AF761395

OECD Economic Surveys: Switzerland 2015

OECD

BETTER POLICIES FOR BETTER LIVES

This document and any map included herein are without prejudice to the status of or sovereignty over any territory, to the delimitation of international frontiers and boundaries and to the name of any territory, city or area.

Please cite this publication as:
OECD (2015), *OECD Economic Surveys: Switzerland 2015*, OECD Publishing, Paris.
http://dx.doi.org/10.1787/eco_surveys-che-2015-en

ISBN 978-92-64-24704-8 (print)
ISBN 978-92-64-24706-2 (PDF)
ISBN 978-92-64-24732-1 (epub)

Series: OECD Economic Surveys
ISSN 0376-6438 (print)
ISSN 1609-7513 (online)

OECD Economic Surveys: Switzerland
ISSN 1995-3402 (print)
ISSN 1999-0464 (online)

The statistical data for Israel are supplied by and under the responsibility of the relevant Israeli authorities. The use of such data by the OECD is without prejudice to the status of the Golan Heights, East Jerusalem and Israeli settlements in the West Bank under the terms of international law.

Photo credits: Cover © Shutterstock/Fulcanelli.

Corrigenda to OECD publications may be found on line at: *www.oecd.org/about/publishing/corrigenda.htm*.

Table of contents

Thematic chapters

Boxes

Tables

Figures

This Survey is published on the responsibility of the Economic and Development Review Committee (EDRC) of the OECD, which is charged with the examination of the economic situation of member countries.

The economic situation and policies of Switzerland were reviewed by the Committee on 21 September 2015. The draft report was then revised in the light of the discussions and given final approval as the agreed report of the whole Committee on 16 October 2015.

The Secretariat's draft report was prepared for the Committee by Petar Vujanovic and Richard Dutu under the supervision of Peter Jarrett. Secretarial assistance was provided by Dacil Kurzweg and Krystel Rakotoarisoa and statistical assistance by Patrizio Sicari.

The previous Survey of Switzerland *was issued in November 2013.*

Information about the latest as well as previous Surveys *and more information about how* Surveys *are prepared is available at* www.oecd.org/eco/surveys.

BASIC STATISTICS OF SWITZERLAND, 2014

(Numbers in parentheses refer to the OECD average)*

LAND, PEOPLE AND ELECTORAL CYCLE

Population (million)	8.2		Population density per km²	198.9	(34.9)
Under 15 (%)	14.1	(18.1)	Life expectancy (years, 2013)	82.9	(80.4)
Over 65 (%)	18.5	(16.0)	Men	80.7	(77.8)
Foreign-born (%, 2012)	27.7		Women	85.0	(83.1)
Latest 5-year average growth (%)	1.2	(0.6)	Latest general election	October 2015	

ECONOMY

Gross domestic product (GDP)			Value added shares (%, 2013)		
In current prices (billion USD)	708.9		Primary sector	0.7	(2.5)
In current prices (billion CHF)	648.0		Industry including construction	25.7	(26.6)
Latest 5-year average real growth (%)	1.9	(1.9)	Services	73.6	(70.7)
Per capita (000 USD PPP)[a]	58.0	(39.2)			

GENERAL GOVERNMENT

Per cent of GDP

Expenditure (2013)	33.5	(41.9)	Gross financial debt[a]	45.8	(110.3)
Revenue (2013)	33.6	(37.7)	Net financial debt[a]	7.0	(68.0)

EXTERNAL ACCOUNTS

Exchange rate (CHF per USD)	0.914		Main exports (% of total merchandise exports)		
PPP exchange rate (USA = 1)	1.361		Chemicals and related products, n.e.s.	29.8	
In per cent of GDP			Commodities and transactions, n.e.s.	25.2	
Exports of goods and services	63.9	(53.6)	Miscellaneous manufactured articles	19.4	
Imports of goods and services	51.9	(49.4)	Main imports (% of total merchandise imports)		
Current account balance	7.0	(0.0)	Commodities and transactions, n.e.s.	26.2	
Net international investment position	116.4		Machinery and transport equipment	19.1	
			Chemicals and related products, n.e.s.	17.7	

LABOUR MARKET, SKILLS AND INNOVATION

Employment rate for 15-64 year-olds (%)	79.9	(65.7)	Unemployment rate, Labour Force Survey (age 15 and over) (%)	4.5	(7.3)
Men	84.5	(73.6)	Youth (age 15-24, %)	8.6	(15.0)
Women	75.2	(57.9)	Long-term unemployed (1 year and over, %)	1.7	(2.5)
Participation rate for 15-64 year-olds (%)	83.8	(71.2)	Tertiary educational attainment 25-64 year-olds (%, 2013)	38.9	(33.3)
Average hours worked per year	1 568	(1 770)	Gross domestic expenditure on R&D (% of GDP, 2012)	3.0	(2.3)

ENVIRONMENT

Total primary energy supply per capita (toe, 2013)	3.3	(4.2)	CO_2 emissions from fuel combustion per capita (tonnes, 2012)	5.1	(9.7)
Renewables (%, 2013)	20.2	(8.8)	Water abstractions per capita (1 000 m^3, 2012)	0.2	
Fine particulate matter concentration (urban, PM^{10}, $\mu g/m^3$, 2011)	20.6	(28.0)	Municipal waste per capita (tonnes, 2013[b])	0.7	(0.5)

SOCIETY

Income inequality (Gini coefficient, 2012)	0.285	(0.308)	Education outcomes (PISA score, 2012)		
Relative poverty rate (%, 2012)	9.1	(10.9)	Reading	509	(496)
Median equivalised household income (000 USD PPP, 2010)	31.3	(20.4)	Mathematics	531	(494)
Public and private spending (% of GDP)			Science	515	(501)
Health care, current expenditure (2013)	11.1	(9.0)	Share of women in parliament (%, July 2015)	28.5	(27.0)
Pensions (2011)	11.8	(8.7)	Net official development assistance (% of GNI)	0.49	(0.36)
Education (primary, secondary, post sec. non tertiary, 2011)	4.0	(3.9)			

Better life index: *www.oecdbetterlifeindex.org/fr/*

* Where the OECD aggregate is not provided in the source database, a simple OECD average of latest available data is calculated where data exist for at least 29 member countries.

a) 2012 for Switzerland.

b) 2012 for the OECD aggregate.

Source: Calculations based on data extracted from the databases of the following organisations: OECD, International Energy Agency, World Bank, International Monetary Fund and Inter-Parliamentary Union.

Abbreviations and acronyms

AEOI	Automatic exchange of information
AI	Invalidity insurance
ALM	Asset and liability management
ANQ	Association nationale pour le développement de la qualité dans les hôpitaux et les cliniques
ARE	Federal office for spatial development
AVS	Assurance vieillesse et survivants
BEPS	Base erosion and profit shifting
BFS	Bureau of federal statistics
BIS	Bank for international settlement
BSV	Federal social insurance office
CAO	Capital adequacy ordinance
CCB	Counter-cyclical buffer
CDIP	Conférence suisse des directeurs de l'instruction publique
CGSO	Conférence des gouvernements de Suisse occidentale
CGTs	Capital gains taxes
CoCos	Contingent convertibles
CPI	Consumer price index
CSRE	Centre suisse de coordination pour la recherche en éducation
DEA	Data envelopment analysis
DRG	Diagnostic-related group
EAER	Federal department of economic affairs, education and research
EFTA	European free trade association
EOI	Exchange of information
ETH Zürich	Eidgenössische technische hochschule zürich
FATF	Financial action task force
FDF	Federal department of finance
FEDRO	Federal roads office
FFA	Federal finance administration
FINMA	Financial market supervisory authority
FIT	Feed-in tariffs
FOAG	Federal office for agriculture
FOEN	Federal office for the environment
FOPH	Federal office of public health
FSI	Financial soundness indicators
FSO	Federal statistical office
FTA	Foreign trade association
GDP	Gross domestic product
GHG	Greenhouse gas

GNI	Gross national income
HAI	Housing affordability index
IRU	International Raiffeisen union
ITS-CH	Intelligent transport system – Switzerland
KOF	Business cycle research centre of EPF Zürich
LAMal	Loi fédérale sur l'assurance-maladie
LTV	Loan-to-value
MCAA	Multilateral competent authority agreement
NZZ	Neue zürcher zeitung
PET	Professional education and training
PISA	Programme for international student assessment
PPP	Purchasing power parity
PPPs	Public-private partnerships
PSEs	Producer support estimates
SAAS	Swiss academy of arts and sciences
SAMS	Swiss academy of medical sciences
SBA	Swiss bankers association
SBB	Schweizerische bundesbahnen
SECO	State secretariat for economic affairs
SFBC	Swiss federal banking commission
SFOE	Swiss federal office of energy
SFOH	Swiss federal office of health
SILC	Statistics on income and living conditions
SNB	Swiss national bank
STEM	Science, technology, engineering and mathematics
STRI	Services trade restrictiveness index
TBTF	Too-big-to-fail
TSE	Total support estimate
UAS	Universities of applied sciences
VET	Vocational education and training
WHO	World health organization
WTO	World trade organisation

Executive summary

- *The economy has performed well, but productivity growth has been weak*
- *Taming the housing market cycle*
- *Improving the efficiency of public spending*

The economy has performed well, but productivity growth has been weak

The economy has been performing well

Real GDP, 2008 Q1 = 100

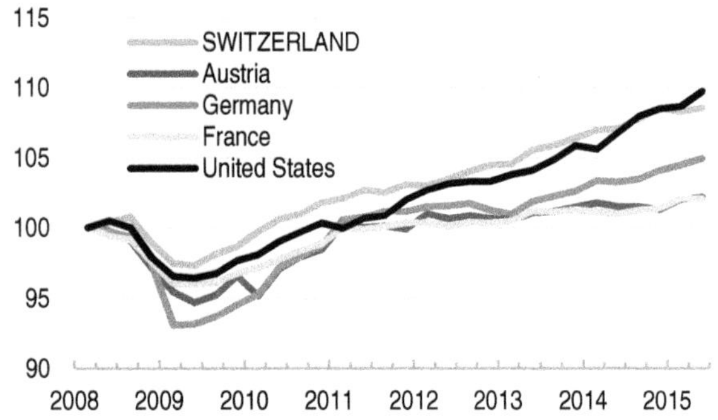

Source: *OECD Economic Outlook 97 Database* (and updates).

StatLink http://dx.doi.org/10.1787/888933292295

Swiss economic growth bounced back strongly after the 2009 recession, underpinned by low interest rates, high immigration and an exchange rate ceiling until early-2015, which supported robust export growth. Inflation has been low or negative over the past four years, due in significant part to the strong currency. Well-being and happiness indicators are high, with low unemployment, ample real wage growth and a relatively even distribution of income. The sharp appreciation following the end of the currency ceiling is hurting short-term growth. A public initiative in February 2014 is set to impose limits on immigration, which will put a premium on stronger productivity growth in the years ahead.

Taming the housing market cycle

Growth in real house prices

% change, 2007 to 2014

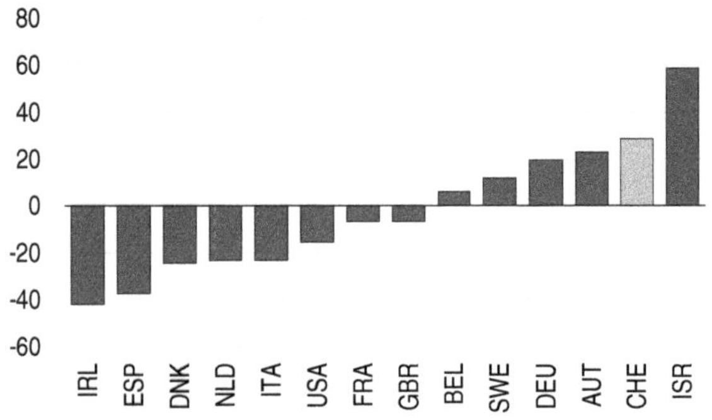

Source: *OECD House Price Database.*

StatLink http://dx.doi.org/10.1787/888933292397

Real estate prices have grown rapidly in recent years, especially in certain hotspots. The residential mortgage debt-to-GDP ratio of 120% is the highest in the OECD, and banks are exposed to the real estate sector. High house prices are being supported by very low interest rates, population growth, and smaller family units. Restrictive planning regulations have limited the increase in supply. Policy measures have relieved pressures somewhat, but to foster a soft landing and avoid unsustainable booms, supply needs to be made more responsive.

Improving the efficiency of public spending

Government spending

As a percentage of GDP, 2014

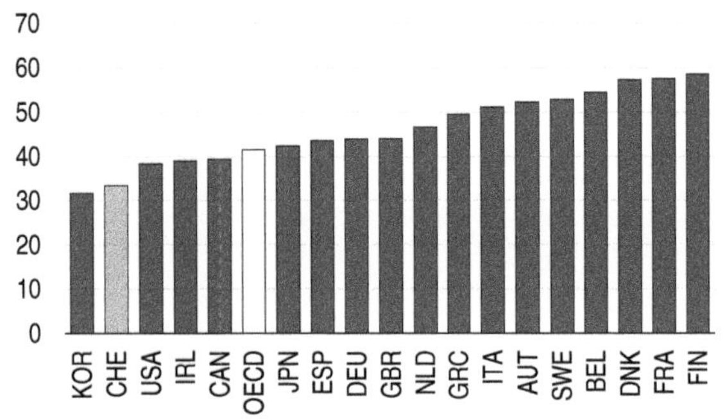

Source: *OECD Economic Outlook 97 Database* (and updates).

StatLink http://dx.doi.org/10.1787/888933292634

Switzerland has a long tradition of small government, which has not hindered its high international ranking in education, health or infrastructure. However, as the population ages the demand for public services will rise and revenues will be squeezed. Reconciling these long-term trends with small government will require an intensified focus on the efficiency of public spending.

MAIN FINDINGS	KEY RECOMMENDATIONS
Macroeconomic policy	
Growth has been strong, but is slowing sharply.	
Policy interest rates are negative, but there is fiscal room under the debt brake.	Retain the debt brake, but allow the automatic stabilisers to operate fully.
Boosting productivity and growth	
Productivity growth has been weak.	
The possibility that immigration will be curtailed means that efforts to improve productivity performance need to be redoubled.	Increase competition in the telecoms and energy sectors, including privatising Swisscom. Push forward with reforms in the agricultural sector. Focus economic policy on measures increasing productivity growth. Extend the network of free-trade agreements, including with India and the United States.
While women participate actively in the labour force and constitute the majority of tertiary graduates, most work only part time.	Take measures to promote more intensive participation of women in the work force such as by increasing the supply of childcare facilities and introducing individual as opposed to family taxation.
The housing market	
Overheating in the housing sector poses a potential threat to the economy.	
The Swiss National Bank (SNB) has been warning of overheating in the housing market for a few years, and several policy measures have been taken to cool activity, including voluntary measures by the commercial banks.	Establish a framework for explicitly addressing affordability risk, to be used if needed to contain financial stability risks related to imbalances in the housing and mortgage markets.
Mortgage lending growth to non-financial corporations has outpaced lending to households.	Monitor closely mortgage lending to firms or households for rental properties, which may not be as responsive as the owner-occupied segment to recent regulatory measures.
Housing investment is low and unresponsive to demand conditions.	Review spatial planning regulations to make it easier to build denser housing. Limit the tax deductibility of mortgage interest so that, combined with maintenance outlays, it does not exceed the amount of declared imputed rent. Update the imputed rent calculations more frequently to better reflect market values.

MAIN FINDINGS	KEY RECOMMENDATIONS
Efficiency of public spending	
The fiscal position is solid, but future spending needs will rise, putting a premium on spending efficiency	
Pupils who have attended pre-primary education for less than a year, or are from a socio-economically disadvantaged background, have significantly lower academic performance.	Increase public spending on early childhood education and care, especially for children with disadvantaged socio-economic backgrounds (including those from immigrant backgrounds), which could be combined with a generalisation of the childcare voucher systems in the Canton of Lucerne.
The high dropout rate in university for students coming from some cantons imposes a cost on the other cantons. In addition, the particularly high dropout rates among some foreign students impose costs on the university system.	Evaluate solutions to reduce the drop-out rate in the university system.
The demand for graduates in science and engineering, health care, teaching and in certain crafts is rising.	Boost the supply and attractiveness of fields of study that are in high demand in the labour market. Further clarify study streams across the tertiary education system.
Generic drugs are on average nearly three times as expensive as in neighbouring countries.	Switch the system for setting generic drug prices to reimbursing a pre-determined fixed amount.
A lack of data hinders the assessment of rates charged by hospitals.	Encourage systematic benchmarking of hospital costs. If rates keep rising despite the recent reforms, consider new legislation to control them using cost benchmarks.
Demographic and aging-related spending pressures will rise.	Fix the retirement age at 65 for both sexes and thereafter link it to life expectancy. To cut early retirement, reduce existing incentives and pay a larger pension premium for those who choose to work longer.
Environmental sustainability	
Switzerland has set itself ambitious targets in its international commitments to climate change abatement.	
The CO_2 levy is unevenly applied across sectors, and exemptions implicitly subsidise CO_2 emissions.	Increase the CO_2 levy, and remove exemptions to this and other green taxes.
	Move forward with linking the Swiss and the EU emissions trading systems.
The nuclear phase-out poses challenges.	Make greater use of market mechanisms to lower the cost of the transition from nuclear to renewable energy. This includes redesigning the current feed-in tariff scheme.

Assessment and recommendations

- *Recent macroeconomic developments and prospects*
- *Boosting medium-term growth prospects*
- *Policies to tame the housing cycle*
- *Raising efficiency in public spending*
- *Adjusting to international best practice on tax issues, including information exchange*

Following a recession in 2009, economic growth in Switzerland bounced back strongly, outpacing its main European trading partners and matching the strength of the US recovery (Figure 1, Panel A). As the recession hit, the Swiss National Bank (SNB) implemented an ultra-low interest rate policy and in 2011 enforced a ceiling on the franc versus the euro. The rebound in growth has been led primarily by exports, which recovered quickly after the 2009 recession (Panel B), and household consumption. Switzerland's performance in terms of per capita GDP growth over the past decade has been near the OECD average, as has its labour productivity performance (Panel C).

Figure 1. **Real GDP growth and its main components**

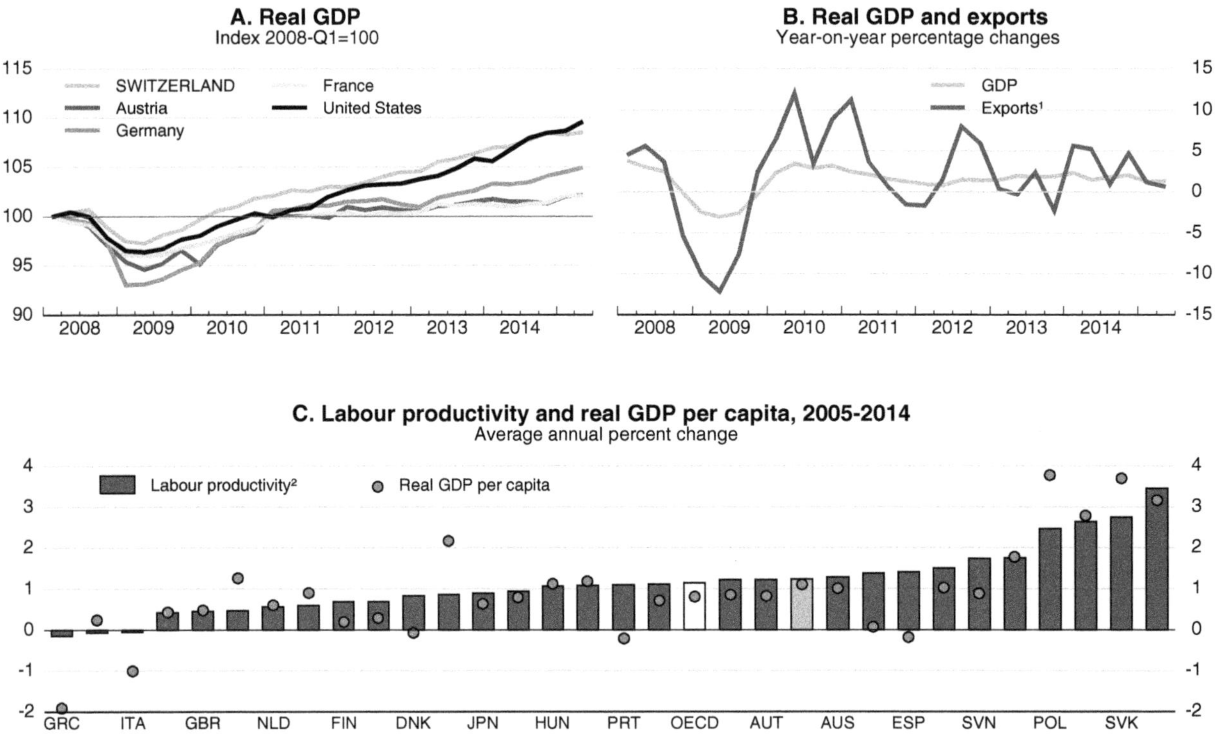

1. Excluding non-monetary gold and valuables.
2. Productivity measured using hours workerd.

Source: *OECD, Economic Outlook 97 Database* (and updates); *OECD National Accounts Database*; and SECO.

StatLink http://dx.doi.org/10.1787/888933292295

Well-being and happiness indicators are also high, with several major Swiss cities regularly ranking among the world's best places to live. In the OECD Better Life Index (Figure 2), all but one of Switzerland's component scores exceeds the OECD average, with particularly high scores in life satisfaction and health. Although Switzerland ranks highly in the provision of basic housing facilities, the high cost of housing drags down the

Figure 2. **The OECD Better Life Index for Switzerland**

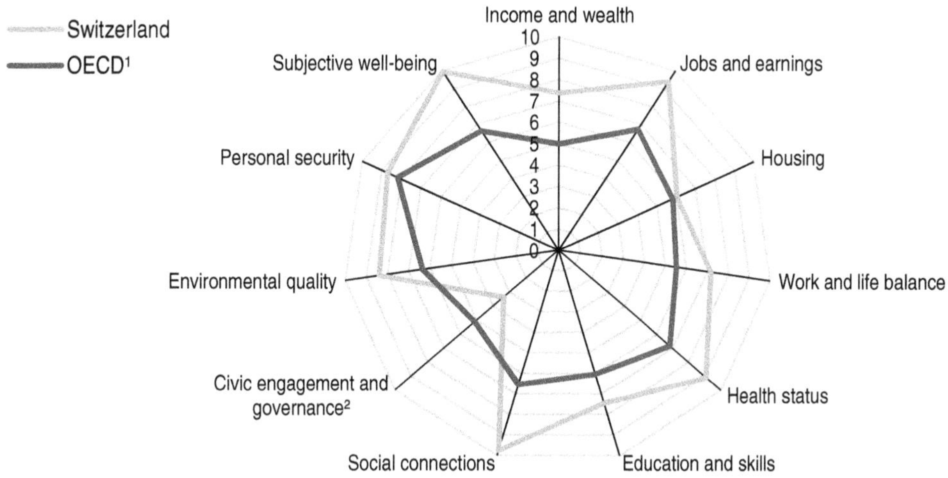

1. Unweighted average.
2. The civic engagement index is partially based on average voter turnout. Direct democracy in Switzerland means that there are a disproportionately large number of national polls, with relatively low average turnout.

Source: OECD Better Life Index, *www.betterlifeinitiative.org*.

StatLink *http://dx.doi.org/10.1787/888933292308*

aggregate score. This issue is discussed in detail in Chapter 2. While the redistributive impact of taxes and transfers is comparatively small, Switzerland remains in the more equal half of OECD countries after taxes and transfers. Even so, inequality in GDP per capita across the regions is high by OECD standards (Demmou et al., 2015).

The dynamic and open Swiss economy is continuing to attract immigrants, and as pointed out in the previous *Survey*, this accounts for a significant part of Switzerland's robust economic growth. In February 2014, a popular initiative on "mass immigration" was passed, which obliges the government to impose quotas on immigration by 2017, including from the European Union. This measure calls into question a key source of Switzerland's growth model and already appears to be weakening confidence. These developments imply that in the medium term growth will have to rely increasingly on productivity gains.

More immediately, the economy was hit with a shock when, on 15 January 2015, the SNB removed the ceiling on the franc, leading to a sharp appreciation, especially against the euro. With almost two-thirds of Swiss exports going to Europe, this exchange rate shock has affected exports and growth, and has been pushing down consumer prices.

Against this backdrop, the key messages of this *Survey* are:

- Switzerland has long benefited from a strong inflow of foreign workers. Restrictions on this inflow means that policy will need to focus on improving productivity performance by allowing resources to be directed to their most productive use. This requires flexible labour and product markets and increased public spending efficiency, as well as liberalisation of the agricultural and energy sectors.
- Real estate prices in Switzerland have grown rapidly in recent years, the residential mortgage debt-to-GDP ratio, at 120%, is the OECD's highest, and banks are very exposed to the property sector, with over 80% domestic of bank loans being mortgages on aggregate. While pressure seems now to be abating, aided by measures taken by banks and authorities over the past three years, policies are needed to make supply more responsive.

- Public expenditure in Switzerland was just 33.5% of GDP in 2014, one of the lowest in the OECD. But as the population ages, demands for public services will rise and revenues will be undermined, calling for improvements in public spending efficiency.

Recent macroeconomic developments and prospects

With GDP contracting 0.2% in the first quarter, economic activity in Switzerland was hit hard by the sharp 15% appreciation of the franc against the euro in early 2015, following the removal of the currency ceiling (Figure 3, Panels A and B). The appreciation put an end to the trade-led momentum in 2014. However, the economy already rebounded by 0.2% in the second quarter, supported by solid domestic demand. The sectoral composition of growth has also switched from consumption-related components to manufacturing (Figure 4, Panel A). As confidence has suffered, demand for credit is at its lowest point in three years even though it is still growing faster than GDP (Figure 4, Panel B). At the same time, Swiss households are making the most of the strong franc, with cross-border shopping up nearly 30% in some places (Bloomberg, 2015).

Falling global oil prices and the currency appreciation resulted in consumer prices falling 1% year-on-year in June 2015 (Figure 4, Panel C). To remain competitive with imports (whose prices fell 4.9% year-on-year in May), Swiss companies have had to cut their prices: the GDP deflator dropped 0.9% in the first quarter. However, as with the 2011 appreciation

Figure 3. **Components of GDP growth and exchange rates**

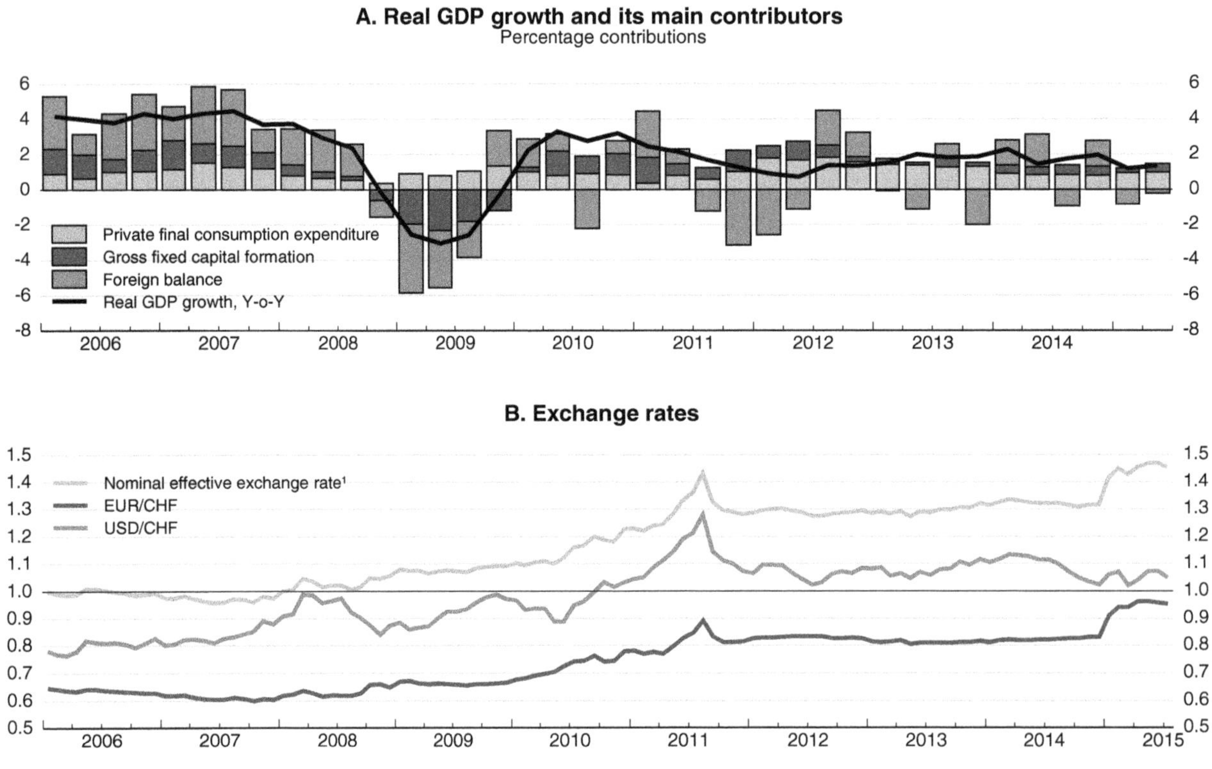

1. *Vis-à-vis* 40 trading partners; January 2006 = 1.

Source: *OECD, Economic Outlook 97 Database* (and updates); SECO; and SNB.

StatLink http://dx.doi.org/10.1787/888933292312

episode, falling prices are the result of the exchange rate pass-through, rather than entrenched deflation expectations, with a majority of households not expecting prices to fall. This is evidenced by the strongly negative contribution of imported goods to CPI inflation (Figure 4, Panel C).

Employment growth picked up to 1.2% year-on-year in the second quarter of 2015. Although the unemployment rate of 4.3% (labour force survey measure) remains low by international standards, some worrying trends are emerging. As the government extended support to short-time work (employees working fewer hours while the government tops up their pay) to include businesses having difficulties resulting from the discontinuation of the exchange rate ceiling, firms doubled their recourse to this measure compared to a year earlier, and more businesses consider current employment levels to be too high than too low (KOF, 2015a). Real wages (deflated by producer prices) grew by 1.6% in 2014 – already in excess of productivity gains of 0.3% – and have accelerated into 2015 (Figure 4, Panel D).

At around 7% of GDP in 2014 and projected to be close to 10% for the first half of 2015, Switzerland's current account surplus is still very large, led by the goods and services balance of 12% of GDP. The contribution from merchanting has flattened off in recent years, but income inflows from licensing fees and research and development services are continuing to surge, together now amounting to over 3% of GDP. With high real unit labour

Figure 4. **Macroeconomic indicators**

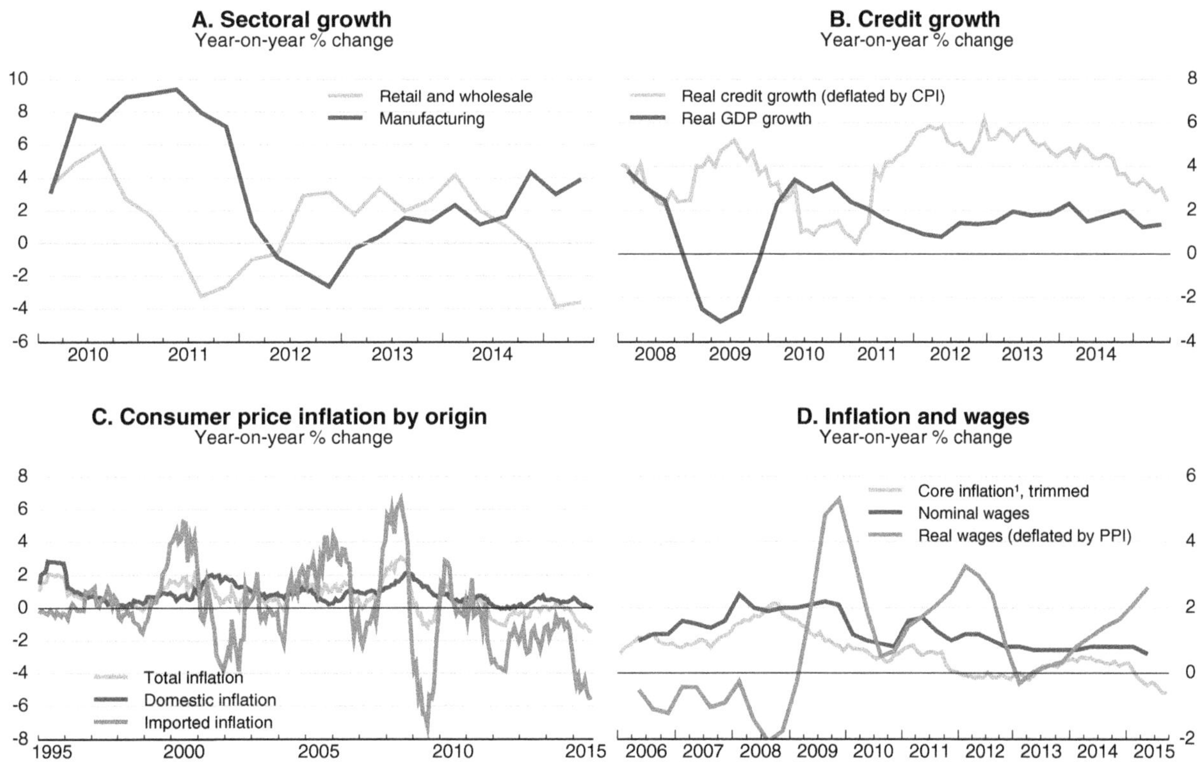

1. The trimmed mean is a measure for core inflation based on a reduced basket of items. It factors out those 15% of items with the highest and those 15% with the lowest annual price increases from the CPI basket.

Source: *OECD, Economic Outlook 97 Database* (and updates); SECO; and SNB.

StatLink http://dx.doi.org/10.1787/888933292326

costs, exporting firms were already operating with thin margins. That said, Swiss exports are heavily concentrated in relatively price-insensitive goods such as pharmaceuticals and watches, so weathering the loss of competitiveness in those industries will be easier (Auer and Sauré, 2011; KOF, 2015b). However, Switzerland continues to underperform with regard to trade (OECD, 2013a), and the authorities should therefore continue to promote trade links, especially with non-European markets, and make progress on extending Switzerland's network of free-trade agreements, including with India and the United States.

Table 1. **Macroeconomic indicators and projections**

	2011	2012	2013	2014	2015	2016
	Current prices CHF billion	Percentage changes, volume (2010 prices)				
GDP at market prices	618.3	1.1	1.8	1.9	0.7	1.1
Private consumption	333.4	2.7	2.2	1.3	1.2	1.5
Government consumption	66.4	2.1	1.3	1.3	2.4	0.6
Gross fixed capital formation	144.6	2.9	1.2	2.1	1.3	1.3
Of which: Business	106.2	3.8	1.4	2.1	0.7	1.1
Housing	19.3	1.5	1.7	1.6	1.0	1.1
Government	19.1	-1.1	-0.7	0.0	0.4	0.5
Final domestic demand	544.4	2.7	1.8	1.5	1.4	1.3
Stockbuilding[1]	21.5	-3.4	-2.5	0.6	-0.8	-0.4
Total domestic demand	565.9	-1.2	-0.9	2.4	2.3	0.9
Exports of goods and services[2]	406.7	1.1	15.2	-6.9	-2.1	0.0
Imports of goods and services[2]	354.3	-2.6	13.4	-8.1	-0.1	-0.6
Net exports[1]	52.4	2.2	2.6	-0.1	-1.3	0.3
Other indicators (% change, unless otherwise specified):						
Potential GDP	-	1.8	1.7	1.6	1.5	1.5
Output gap[3]	-	-1.0	-0.9	-0.6	-1.4	-1.7
Employment	-	1.2	1.1	1.5	1.5	1.0
Unemployment rate[4]	-	4.1	4.3	4.4	4.3	4.3
GDP deflator	-	-0.2	0.0	-0.7	-1.0	-0.3
Consumer price index	-	-0.7	-0.2	0.0	-1.2	-0.5
Core consumer prices	-	-1.0	-0.2	0.1	-0.4	-0.2
Household saving ratio, net[5]	-	18.7	19.0	18.2	17.7	16.9
Trade balance[6]	-	10.4	12.1	11.3	10.9	11.3
Current account balance[6]	-	10.3	11.1	7.3	9.8	9.9
General government fiscal balance[6]	-	0.2	-0.3	-0.2	-0.3	-0.4
Underlying government fiscal balance[3]	-	0.1	0.2	-0.2	0.0	0.1
Underlying government primary fiscal balance[3]	-	0.5	0.5	0.0	0.2	0.2
General government gross debt[6]	-	45.8	46.0	46.2	46.5	46.8
General government net debt[6]	-	7.1	7.3	7.4	7.7	8.0
Three-month money market rate, average	-	0.1	0.0	0.0	-0.8	-0.7
Ten-year government bond yield, average	-	0.6	0.9	0.7	0.0	0.1

1. Contributions to changes in real GDP, actual amount in the first column.
2. On 30 September 2014 the Swiss authorities published revised figures for the national accounts in compliance with ESA 2010. Revised export and import data now include non-monetary gold and merchanting, which are more volatile. Together with valuables, they accounted for nearly half of exports in 2013-14.
3. As a percentage of potential GDP.
4. As a percentage of the labour force.
5. As a percentage of household disposable income.
6. As a percentage of GDP.

Source: OECD Economic Outlook 97 Database (and updates).

Monetary policy has been expansionary, with near-zero policy rates since 2009 and the currency ceiling against the euro between mid-2011 and the beginning of 2015, and more recently, negative interest rates. That said, given persistent negative inflation, real policy rates have not been as expansionary as nominal rates would suggest. In late 2014, to defend the currency ceiling the SNB had to intervene again in foreign exchange markets resulting in rapid reserve accumulation and SNB balance-sheet expansion (Figure 5, Panel A). In December 2014 foreign currency reserves jumped almost 7% (5% of GDP) due to interventions and significant valuation effects. Given the expected divergence in the trajectories of monetary policy between the United States and euro area, the exchange rate ceiling was deemed to be unsustainable and was abandoned in January 2015. Simultaneously the SNB cut rates further, charging 0.75% on all deposits with it that exceed a specific exemption threshold (Figure 5, Panel B). For domestic banks the threshold currently corresponds to 20 times the minimum reserve requirement and is adjusted to the amount of cash held. For other account holders the threshold is CHF 10 million.

Figure 5. **Monetary policy has been stimulative**

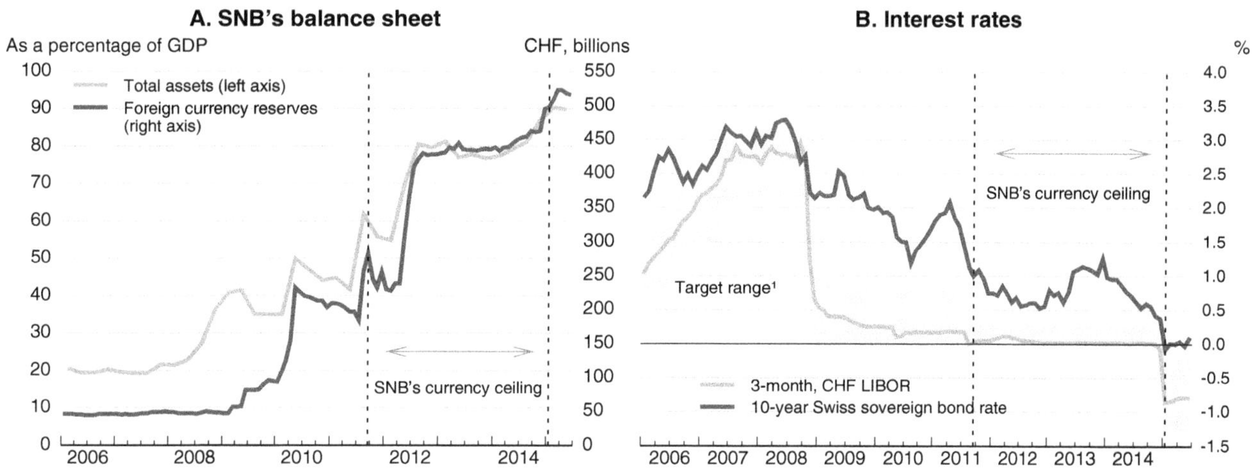

1. The SNB implements its monetary policy by fixing a target range for the three-month Swiss franc Libor. The Libor is a reference interest rate in the interbank market for unsecured loans. It is a trimmed mean of the rates charged by 11 leading banks and is published daily by the International Commodities Exchange (ICE).

Source: Swiss National Bank, *Monthly Statistical Bulletin* and *Monthly Bulletin of Banking Statistics*, August 2015; and *OECD Economic Outlook 97 Database* (and updates).

StatLink http://dx.doi.org/10.1787/888933292338

Given the long period of very low or negative inflation, such expansionary policy is appropriate. However, the unintended consequences of negative interest rates are becoming more evident. For example, pension funds that were already finding it difficult to reach their legal target returns on portfolios are struggling even more. While negative interest rates could make real estate investment even more attractive and thus risk cancelling out the effect of recent macro-prudential measures (see below), mortgages rates have not fully reflected the change in the policy rate. Negative or very low positive rates may also lead to low-quality investment in other assets. Furthermore, at some point, individuals and institutions may respond by holding cash rather than bank deposits (a "rush to cash") even though there have been few signs of this as yet. The SNB should evaluate how low interest rates can go and for how long.

Immediately after the exchange rate ceiling was abandoned in January 2015, the Swiss franc appreciated dramatically against the euro but then settled at around 1.05 which constituted a 12.5% appreciation. Since September the franc has weakened to around 1.09 to the euro as volatility in markets declined, safe haven effects abated and the interest rate differential effect became important (Figure 3, Panel B).

Fiscal policy remains broadly neutral. Due to lower-than-expected revenues from direct taxes, a federal deficit emerged in 2014 for the first time since 2005, though the general government remained in small surplus. Federal government gross debt is only 45% of GDP and there is room under the debt break. Therefore, the automatic stabilisers should be allowed to play fully as the economy absorbs the exchange rate shock.

Stability of the financial sector

The banking sector is large relative to GDP and is dominated by two big banks, UBS and Credit Suisse, which together hold approximately half of all banking assets. The 2012 *Survey* included a special chapter on the financial system and made a number of recommendations to reduce the risks that the sector poses to the broader economy. Since then progress has been steady. In the past couple of years the two big banks have improved their capital position and now meet most requirements of the Swiss "too-big-to-fail" regulations and the international Basel III framework, both of which will apply fully from 2019. Given perceptions of continuing risks, prudential requirements are currently being reviewed by both domestic authorities and international bodies which may result in more stringent requirements.

Risks to financial stability remain, however. The two big banks must remain well capitalised, among others to withstand a downturn in real estate prices (see below) as well as other more general risks, both domestic and foreign in origin such as those related to exchange rate volatility. However, while their risk-weighted asset ratios and leverage ratios are at or above target, the latter are below average in international comparison. Given the ultra-low interest rates, increased imbalances in real estate markets now appear more likely, as such investment has become increasingly attractive for investors, further exposing banks to the sector. Already at the end of 2014, UBS and Credit Suisse had domestic loans outstanding totalling CHF 323 billion, 82% of which in the form of mortgage loans (SNB, 2015). At the same time, negative interest rates, the end of banking secrecy and meeting domestic and international regulatory requirements, are likely to weigh on revenues. Swiss authorities are currently considering higher leverage ratios for the bigger banks.

Growth is expected to recover in 2016

After contracting in the first quarter of 2015, reflecting the impact of the exchange rate appreciation, activity rebounded already in the second quarter on the back of solid consumption and investment growth and a rebound in goods and services exports. The discontinuation of the ceiling on the Swiss franc (on January 15 this year) is therefore having a limited impact on the economy so far. Annual growth is projected to reach 0.7% for 2015 and accelerate to 1.1% in 2016 (Table 1). Higher real wage gains, lower oil prices and ultra-low interest rates will support consumption in the coming quarters. Rising growth in the EU should also help the export sector offset part of the negative competitiveness effect of the appreciation. The partial reversal of the currency appreciation in recent months will also support the economy moving forward.

Developments in the rest of Europe (including the repercussions from the current refugee crisis) and ripples from the slowdown in China and weakness in other emerging markets could once again affect the exchange rate (up or down) and could change the short-term outlook significantly. In particular, a further appreciation following renewed concerns about the euro area, or geopolitical tensions, could harm growth prospects and extend the duration of negative inflation. With interest rates so negative, sustained housing investment increases could also fuel overheating concerns, especially given the high level of household indebtedness and banks' exposure to the mortgage market (see below). The negative implications of the implementation of the popular initiative against mass immigration, including the possible abrogation of the associated treaties with the European Union, may be significant.

Recommendation for macroeconomic policies

- Retain the debt brake, but allow the automatic stabilisers to operate fully.

Boosting medium-term growth prospects

The level of per capita GDP in Switzerland is above the OECD average (Figure 6, Panel A), but rather than being underpinned by superior levels of labour productivity, it is high labour utilisation that is responsible (Panel B). The labour force participation rate is 84%, unemployment is low (4.5% in 2014) and the proportion of the working-age population in work is high (80%). With the possibility that immigration will be curtailed in 2017 and demographic ageing, the focus of economic policy needs to shift more to promoting productivity growth, exploiting remaining underutilised labour resources, including women (who participate in the labour market but tend to work only part-time), improving educational outcomes and better integrating first-and second-generation immigrants. The business environment could also be improved, particularly by reducing regulatory burdens. Some sectors of the economy could be more exposed to competition, including the telecommunications and agricultural sectors. Challenges posed by climate change need to be tackled, including those posed by the transition out of nuclear power to renewable sources of energy (as discussed in detail in the previous *Survey*).

Productivity issues

Real wages have risen sharply over the past several years, squeezing firms' profits (Figure 7). In contrast, labour productivity per hour, which is comparatively high in level terms, has been relatively stagnant. Part of this disappointing productivity performance may be related to the rising share of low-productivity sectors in job creation: public and semi-public employment was up 25% between 2003 and 2013, versus overall gains of 15%.

As discussed in the previous *Survey*, a number of OECD countries, including Australia, Chile, Denmark, Mexico, and New Zealand have productivity commissions that act as review and advisory bodies on microeconomic policy reform and regulation, with the aim of achieving better informed and motivated policy decisions through independent, published analysis and advice. However, Switzerland already relies heavily on expert commissions and other public consultation exercises and establishing such an independent body may be problematic given the political framework. A report entitled

Figure 6. **GDP per capita is one of the highest in the OECD due to high labour resource utilisation, 2013**

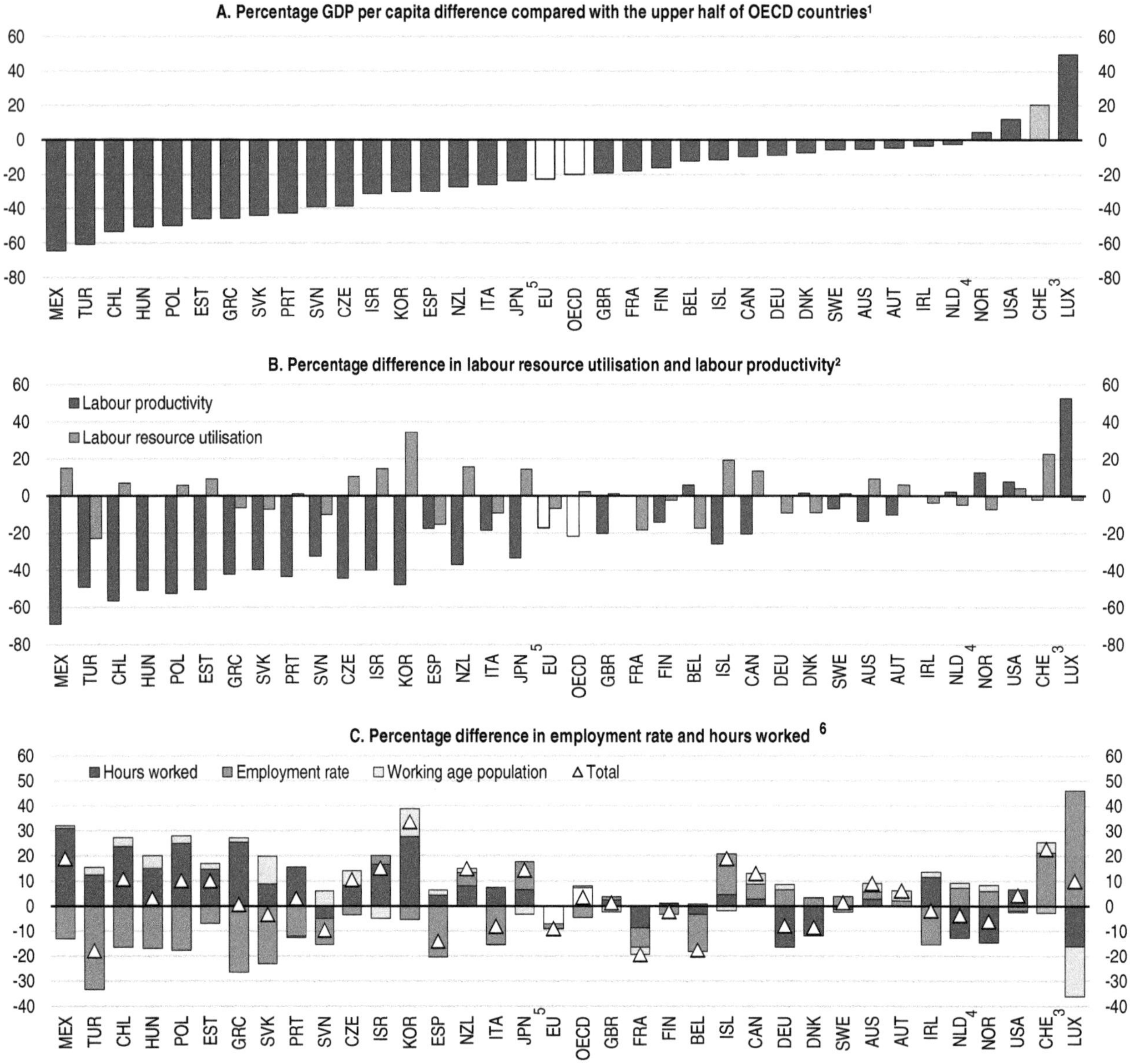

1. Compared to the simple average of the 17 OECD countries with highest GDP per capita in 2013 based on 2013 purchasing power parities (PPPs). The sum of the percentage difference in labour resource utilisation and labour productivity do not add up exactly to the GDP per capita difference since the decomposition is multiplicative.
2. Labour productivity is measured as GDP per hour worked. Labour resource utilisation is measured as the total number of hours worked per capita.
3. In the case of Luxembourg, the population is augmented by the number of cross-border workers in order to take into account their contribution to GDP.
4. Data refer to GDP for mainland Norway which excludes petroleum production and shipping. While total GDP overestimates the sustainable income potential, mainland GDP slightly underestimates it since returns on the financial assets held by the petroleum fund abroad are not included.
5. Average of European Union countries in the OECD.
6. Employment rate is measured as total number of employed people divided by working-age population. Hours worked are measured as total number of hours worked per employed person. Working-age population is measured as working-age population divided by total population. The total of the three components is not exactly equal to labour resource utilisation as presented in panel B since the decomposition is multiplicative.

Source: OECD, *Going for Growth 2015*.

StatLink http://dx.doi.org/10.1787/888933292349

"Principles for a New Growth Policy" was published by the government in January 2015 – the fourth in a series of quadrennial studies on productivity and other economic challenges (SECO, 2015). Examination of productivity issues should be institutionalised to better focus policymaking on raising productivity.

Figure 7. **Real hourly wages have decoupled from labour productivity growth**

Index, 2008-Q1 = 100

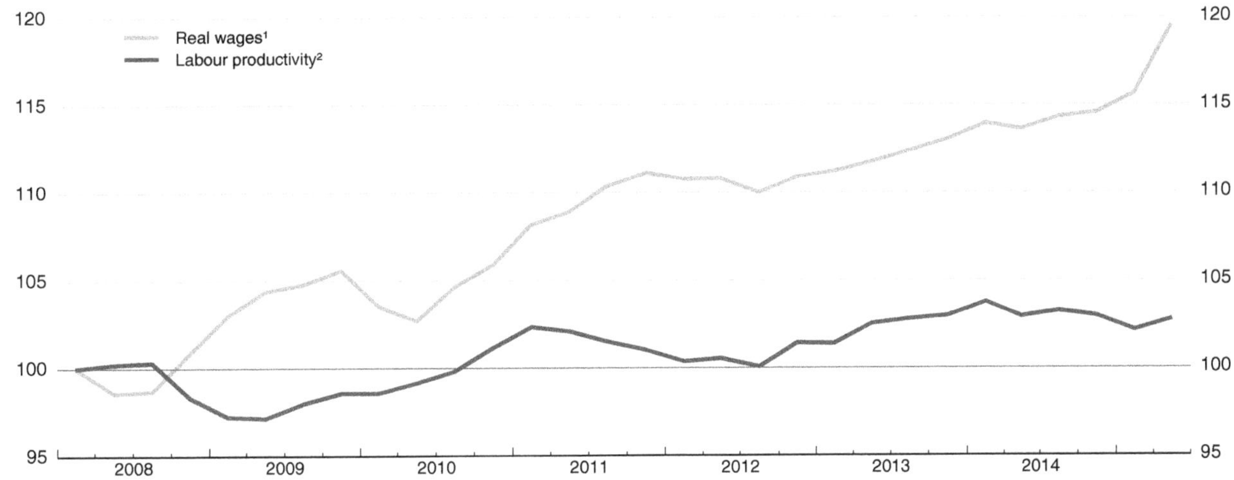

1. Deflated by PPI.
2. Productivity measured using hours worked.

Source: *OECD, Economic Outlook 97 Database* (and updates).

StatLink http://dx.doi.org/10.1787/888933292356

The latest tranche of reforms to the corporate tax system (Corporate Tax Reform III), currently before parliament, appropriately seek to strengthen Switzerland's competiveness as a business location and includes measures such as introducing patent boxes (see below). Implementation needs to be expedited as delays are adding to business uncertainty. More could also be done to improve the regulatory environment, including by allowing businesses to compete even in segments of the economy heretofore considered the preserve of the public sector. This includes electricity generation and transmission, telecoms and postal services. Moreover, greater competition could be promoted by opening up sectors such as agriculture, public health, public procurement and protected professions, all of which have been insulated from competition. Previous *Surveys* have discussed these issues in detail.

While Switzerland performs at around the OECD average in terms of the restrictiveness of its product market regulation, the 2013 index shows that it ranks poorly in the domain of state control – 28th out of 33. Switzerland's mobile telecommunications sector remains the most concentrated of the 24 OECD countries studied by Sung (2014). While provision of utilities is more costly in a small economy like Switzerland, the stringency of the regulation of ownership in these sectors is well above that of other similarly sized countries such as Austria (Figure 8, Panel A). Rules that favour public ownership are particularly rigid in post, telecoms and energy. For instance, Swisscom, which enjoys a 59% market share in mobile communications (the second highest market share for a single telecoms company in the OECD) and 70% of fixed line market, is legally limited to a maximum outside ownership of 49.9% (Swisscom, 2014; OECD, 2013b).

Swisscom is 51% owned by the Swiss Confederation and the government continues to define the company's strategic goals including universal service obligations. In June 2007, the Communication Commission (ComCom) designated Swisscom as a Universal Service Provider thereby obliging the company to provide universal services nationwide for the period 2008 to 2017. The public control of Swisscom raises questions of governance and potential conflicts of interest, and an unfairly lower cost of capital given that it might be seen that Swisscom enjoys an implicit government guarantee (Standard and Poor's, 2015; Moody's, 2012). More needs to be done to increase competition in the critical telecoms and energy sectors, including going ahead with the privatisation of Swisscom.

Increasing the efficiency of the business insolvency regime could further facilitate structural change, thereby directing economic resources away from shrinking and toward emerging sectors (OECD, 2015b). Switzerland ranks rather poorly in terms of debt-recovery rates and the average time it takes to settle insolvencies (Figure 8, Panel B). That said, a number of recent reforms have made resolving insolvencies easier. This included introducing a moratorium period while the debtor is preparing a reorganisation agreement. Nevertheless, the authorities should make greater efforts to streamline insolvency procedures by reducing the time required to implement an insolvency or restructure, and to lift recovery rates.

Figure 8. **Public ownership of telecommunications and utilities, and insolvency in the OECD**

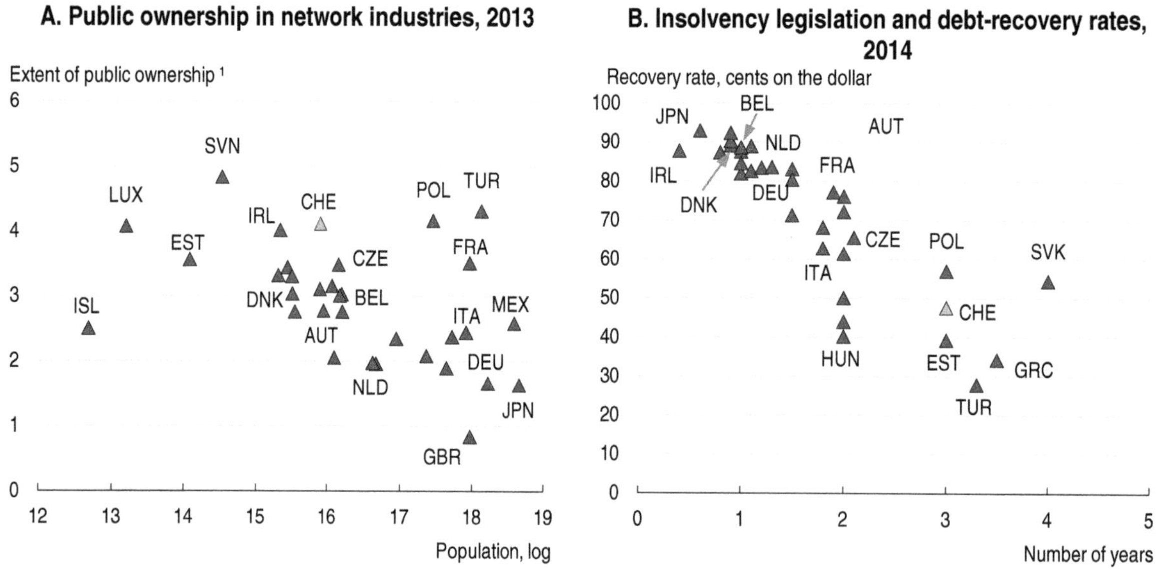

1. Index scale of 0 to 6, from lower to higher levels of public ownership.

Source: *OECD Product Market Regulation Database; OECD National Accounts Database; and World Bank Doing Business Database.*

StatLink http://dx.doi.org/10.1787/888933292360

Services trade leads to the exchange of ideas and technology and helps firms to exploit potential scale economies (by, for example, participating in global value chains), thereby lowering costs and boosting competitiveness. However, Switzerland's services trade regime is relatively restrictive. The Services Trade Restrictiveness Index (STRI) shows that Swiss trade and investment barriers and domestic regulations impede trade in many services sectors. Switzerland's STRI is above the OECD average in 13 of the 17 sectors for which data are available and is particularly restrictive in accounting, legal, broadcasting, courier and computer services.

As noted in the 2011 *Survey*, the Swiss tax system is heavily geared towards the taxation of household income, which is more harmful to economic activity than taxation of consumption, which is low in Switzerland. In addition, complexities related to the many VAT exemptions are burdensome for businesses and should be removed by moving to a single VAT rate. Options to apply the VAT to financial services should also be explored in order to avoid favourable treatment of this sector. As part of plans to better fund the first pillar of the pension system, the Parliament is discussing an increase of the VAT rate.

As discussed in the previous *Survey*, significant productivity gains could be made in the agricultural sector. As an illustration, if the surplus labour could be shifted to the rest of the economy, the output of the whole economy could rise by nearly 3% if used according to best practice, or more than 1% if only an average level of relative productivity is assumed (OECD, 2012). While the shift from price support to direct payments has reduced distortions in agriculture, direct payments still represent nearly two-thirds of the agricultural contribution (0.7%) to the Swiss GDP (648 billion CHF), leaving just one third from valued-added. Barriers to trade also weigh on production efficiency, with tariff protection averaging 32% for agricultural products, versus 1.4% in Australia and 9% in the United States (WTO, 2013, 2014 and 2015). Spending efficiency could be raised by making some of the general direct payment conditional on implementing productivity-enhancing methods and on increasing the share of revenues coming from market activities.

Demographic issues

In recent years the Agreement on the Free Movement of Persons with the EU, which entered into force in 2002, has allowed strong inflows of high-skilled migrants, many coming from Germany (Box 1). But this growth model based on strong employment increases and correspondingly weak productivity gains is now jeopardised by the passing of the February 2014 public initiative against "mass immigration".

Medium-term growth prospects could be boosted by better utilising female labour resources. As pointed out in the last *Survey*, Swiss women have one of the highest participation rates in the OECD, but also one of the lowest levels of average hours worked (OECD, 2013c). The lack and high cost of childcare options, as well as burdensome marginal income tax rates, create disincentives to work more. It is also unhelpful for women wishing to start businesses or take up leadership positions in companies. In addition, with comparable qualifications and experience, men still get paid 7% more than women for the same job. Removing those distortions and boosting the supply of childcare could boost female labour supply. Given that young Swiss women are now on average more educated than their male counterparts, it could also boost productivity.

Climate change issues

Switzerland has low greenhouse gas (GHG) emissions per capita compared to other countries, which reflects its strong reliance on low-emissions energy sources, especially nuclear and hydroelectricity, and its lack of heavy industry. GHG emissions have remained almost unchanged since 1990, as increases from the transport sector have been offset by reductions in the residential and industrial sectors (Figure 10). Because of technical progress, the average CO_2 emitted by new passenger cars fell by one third between 1996 and 2013 (FSO, 2014), but this was offset by higher transport volumes so that emissions from passenger cars actually rose slightly. In 2013, transport accounted for 31% of emissions, ahead of industry (22%) and buildings (29%; 20% from housing).

Box 1. The popular initiative against mass immigration

Switzerland has relied heavily on foreign labour for many decades. Traditionally this has been seasonal and unskilled labour in the construction and tourism sectors, but more recently skilled workers have also been attracted to Switzerland. Currently, annual net migration and the stock of foreign-born residents represent 0.9% and 28% of the population respectively, both among the highest rates in the OECD. In 2010, 63% of foreign-born residents were from EU27 countries, up from 58% in 2000, with lower numbers from Italy and Spain offset by increases from Germany and Portugal (Figure 9). This large inflow of migrants into Switzerland from EU countries was facilitated by the Agreement on the Free Movement of Persons, which came into force in mid-2002. The right of free movement is complemented by the mutual recognition of professional qualifications, by the right to buy property and by the co-ordination of social security systems. The same rules also apply to citizens of EFTA member states.

Figure 9. Foreign-born population by origin, 2000 and 2010

Thousands

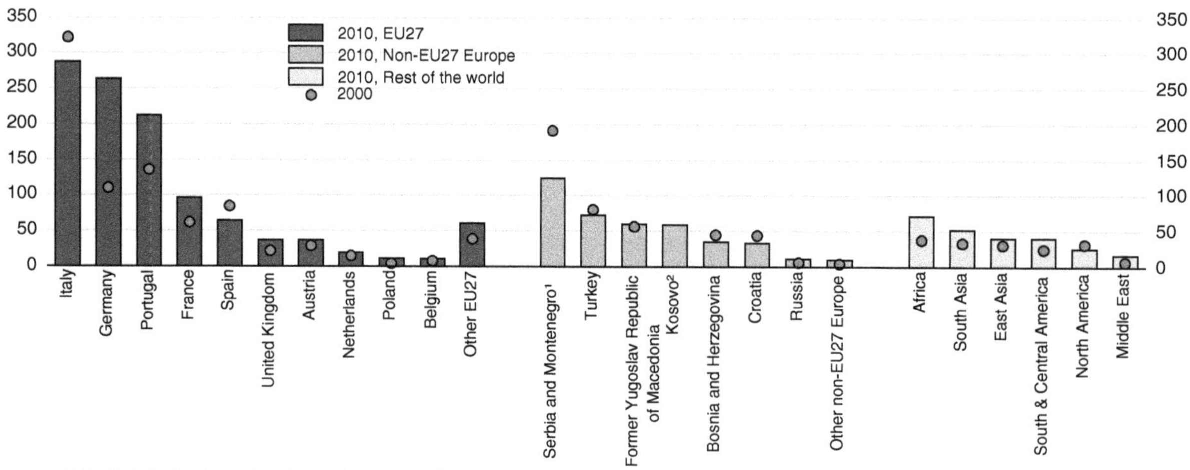

1. The 2010 data are aggregate data from Montenegro and Serbia.
2. 2000 data for Kosovo unavailable.

Source: Swiss Federal Statistical Office.

StatLink http://dx.doi.org/10.1787/888933292375

On 9 February 2014, a vote on a popular initiative (the "Mass Immigration Initiative") aimed at restricting immigration was passed by a narrow margin. The initiative mandates the re-introduction of quotas for almost all immigration categories and imposes limits on foreigners' ability to bring their family members to live in Switzerland, to access Swiss social security benefits and to request asylum. The deadline for implementing this is 2017. When implemented and if re-negotiation with the EU fails, the 1999 Agreement on the Free Movement of Persons with the EU might be abrogated. This agreement forms part of a package of seven co-dependent treaties (the "Bilateral I" package) that also deal with technical obstacles to trade, public procurement, agriculture, research, civil aviation and overland transport. All seven expire if any one of them is abrogated (the "Guillotine Rule"). Because the EU is Switzerland's largest trading partner and a source of skilled migration, this poses a serious risk to the Swiss economy. In July 2014 the EU turned down a request from the Swiss government for a renegotiation of the treaties. However, negotiations with the EU are ongoing with regards to the legislative implementation of the referendum. In November 2014 a popular initiative aimed at reversing the "Mass Immigration Initiative" got underway, but this process can take up to three and a half years.

Recommendations for boosting productivity and medium-term growth

Key recommendations

- Increase competition in the telecoms and energy sectors, including privatising Swisscom.
- Push forward with reforms in the agricultural sector.
- Focus economic policy on measures increasing productivity growth.
- Extend the network of free-trade agreements, including with India and the United States.
- Take measures to promote more intensive participation of women in the work force such as by increasing the supply of childcare facilities and introducing individual as opposed to family taxation.

Other recommendations

- Move to a single VAT rate with as few exemptions as possible.
- Streamline insolvency procedures to facilitate more efficient business adjustment to structural change.

Figure 10. **GHG emissions by sector and targets in Switzerland**

Millions tonnes CO_2 equivalent

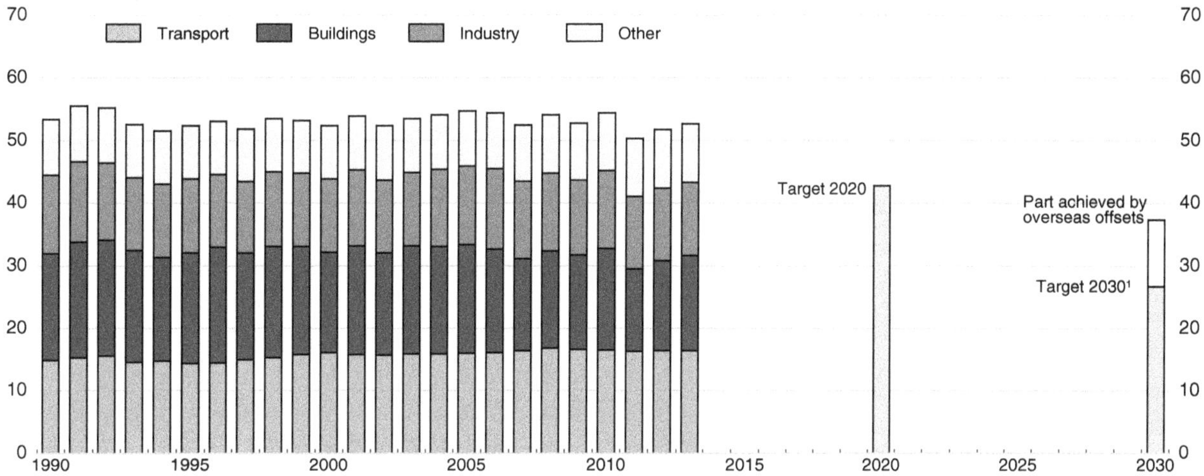

1. The target of 50% below the 1990 levels by 2030 stipulates that at least 30% be achieved domestically, and the remainder achieved by overseas offsets.

Source: Swiss Federal Office for the Environment (FOEN).

StatLink http://dx.doi.org/10.1787/888933292382

Given Switzerland's already low emissions levels, its estimated marginal abatement costs are relatively high, and so meeting its 2020 target of a 20% emissions reduction below the 1990 level will not be easy. The bulk of the emission cuts are expected to come from buildings. One of the main measures is a CO_2 levy on thermal fuels (heating oil and natural gas), the revenues of which are redistributed to the households and the business community. One third (max. CHF 300 million) is earmarked for the buildings programme, which promotes refurbishments and renewable energies and CHF 25 million per year go to a technology fund. CO_2 intensive industries are exempt from the CO_2 levy, if they commit to reducing emissions in return. Large installations are covered by an emissions-trading scheme. Measures regarding transport fuels are CO_2 limits for passenger cars and duties on imports of transport fuels.

In February 2015 the government announced that it aims to reduce Switzerland's GHG emissions to 50% of 1990 levels by 2030, with at least 30% achieved domestically and the rest through purchasing foreign offsets. In order to meet these targets, in addition to what is already planned, more cost-effective initiatives will be needed. Implicit tax rates vary widely across sectors. Taking into account the mineral oil tax, they seem particularly high for transport (though with some exemptions for off-road and public transport), but are not explicitly a CO_2 levy. Depending on the valuation of the non-CO_2 external costs of transport, cost-effective emissions reduction may need much higher taxation on emissions outside transport, even though transport emissions are rising fast. This could be combined with the introduction of a variable congestion charge that would be higher in geographic areas under stress and during peak demand periods to help deal with other external costs of increasing use of road transport.

The use of subsidies and feed-in tariffs (FIT) may not be the best way to encourage the switch to renewable energy sources. The FIT scheme, introduced in 2009, pays producers higher prices over a period of 20 to 25 years and is funded by a levy on all electricity. In 2015 a number of refinements were made to this scheme, including a one-off investment grant for very small producers like households, which will cover up to 30% of the costs of a new installation. However, the cost overhang of the long-term payment commitment inherent in FIT schemes needs to be avoided or at least minimised. Instead of using a FIT, Switzerland should move to solutions that are more responsive to changing market conditions including using tendering in allocating feed-in subsidies and feed-in premiums.

Raising the cost of CO_2 emissions in the household sector is necessary, but the impact can be limited if information is not easily available and the dwelling ownership structure inhibits the incentive effects of price signals. Existing regulations concerning energy-saving renovations of rented dwellings could be better designed, including redefining how costs should be passed on to renters and the compulsory provision of information on the energy efficiency of rental properties (SFOE and SFOH, 2015). Mitigation in the industrial sector would be more cost-effective if the intended linking of the Swiss and the EU emissions trading systems goes ahead; bringing transport fuel (including refineries and importers) into this system would be even more effective. Implicit subsidies to carbon emissions through specific exemptions to the CO_2 levy and other charges should be rationalised.

Recommendations for climate change

Key recommendations

- Increase the CO_2 levy, and remove exemptions to this and other green taxes
- Move forward with linking the Swiss and the EU emissions trading systems.
- Make greater use of market mechanisms to lower the cost of the transition from nuclear to renewable energy. This includes redesigning the current feed-in tariff scheme.

Policies to tame the housing cycle

By some measures, between 2000 and 2014, the average price of apartments in Switzerland almost doubled, and that of single-family homes rose by around 60%. Price increases have been particularly rapid since 2007. Within the OECD only Israel has had larger real house price increases over this period (Figure 11, Panel A). That said, the current

Figure 11. **Real house price and rent indicators**

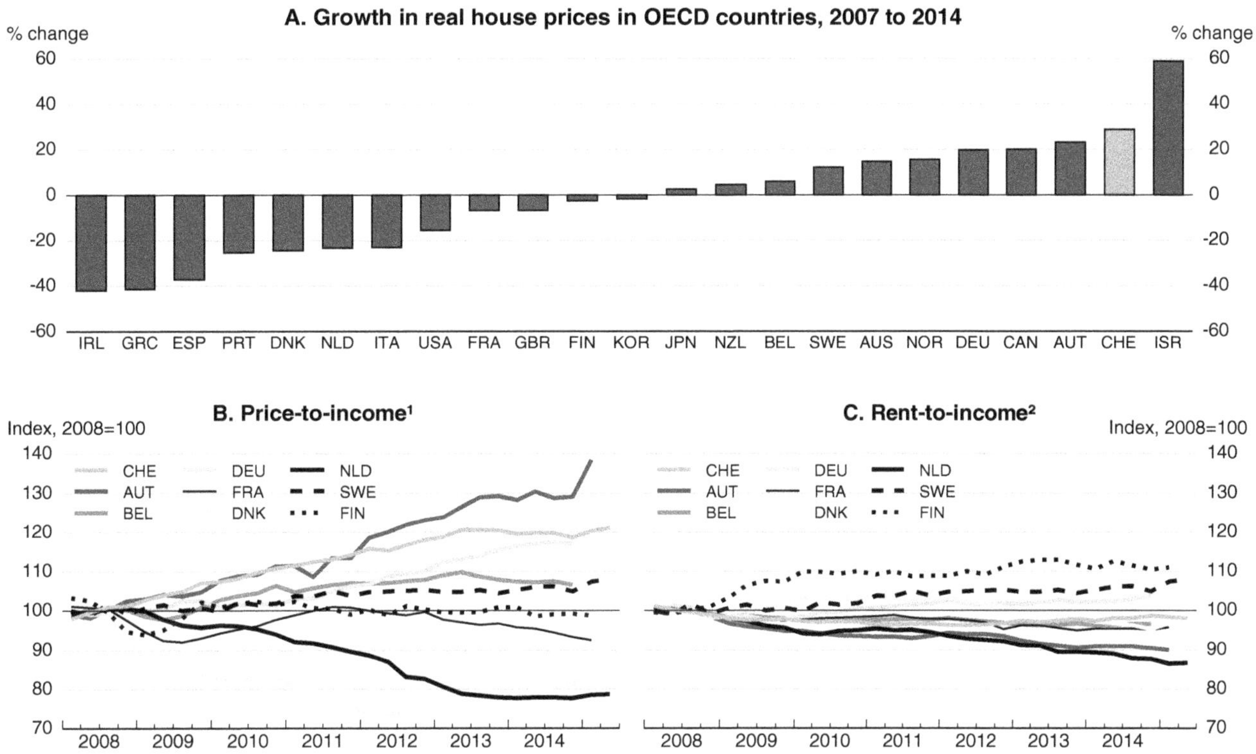

1. Nominal house prices divided by per capita nominal disposable income.
2. Nominal rent prices divided by per capita nominal disposable income.

Source: OECD House Price Database.

StatLink http://dx.doi.org/10.1787/888933292397

house price cycle has been considerably more modest in amplitude than its two predecessors that ended in 1974 and 1989. This rapid rise in prices is reflected in Switzerland's price-to-income ratio, which has increased more quickly since 2008 than in most neighbouring countries (Panel B), suggesting worsening affordability. In contrast, its rent-to-income ratio has been flat over the past decade, reflecting the role of rent controls (Panel C; see Chapter 2).

In Switzerland, tenant protection from abusive rents is a constitutional right. Apartments that come onto the market for the first time are exempt from rent control and the level of rent is determined by market forces, even though the tenant has recourse to subsequently contest the rent. As soon as the lease has been signed, tenancy law takes over, and the rent can be adjusted for inflation, the reference interest rate and other cost factors. After the contract ends, the owner can raise the rent for the next tenant to the local market level, which can again be disputed, and the landlord has to prove compliance with the law. One of the parameters considered is the rent prevailing in neighbouring residences. In times of high demand for rental apartments, the tenancy laws can lead to market distortions, as market rents increase much faster than ongoing contract rents. Long-term tenants therefore have no incentive to move even if the quality and size of their current apartment surpass their needs. These lock-in effects can prolong housing shortages. One solution would be applying differentiated rent-setting rules when large residences are occupied by few people, although such a formula should take into account the ability of low-income households to pay for moving. Moreover, broader deregulation of the tenancy laws would possibly lead to higher rents, harming low-income groups. To support them, targeted housing allowances and/or more social housing would be needed.

Although Swiss households' net wealth is very high, they are among the most indebted in the OECD and have become more so over the past decade. In 2013 gross household debt in Switzerland reached 200% of disposable income, with mortgages making up over 92% of all household financial liabilities. The flipside of highly leveraged households is banks' exposure to the real estate market through mortgage lending. Their exposure is the sixth highest in the OECD, with mortgages on aggregate making up around 84% of all domestic bank loans excluding interbank credit.

The large urban areas like Geneva, Zurich and Basel have experienced the biggest price increases. Indeed, between 2007 and 2014 the price of apartments in Geneva increased by over 70% and those in Zurich by around 50%. Price rises for single-family homes have been more modest and the larger gains concentrated more in the less densely populated urban-satellite cantons such as Zug, Lucerne and Fribourg. Transactions activity has also been robust, with growth in mortgage volumes strongly outpacing income gains.

Since 2010 growth in mortgage lending to non-financial corporations has averaged around 6% per annum while for households it has averaged only 4.5% (Figure 12). While mortgage lending growth to both groups has trailed off substantially since the end of 2012, increases in mortgage lending to both remains above long-term historical averages. This mirrors what happened during the late-1980s housing boom and subsequent banking crisis in Switzerland, during which non-financial corporations became overextended as the economy slowed and house prices began to fall. Moreover, despite having increased somewhat over the past few years, the private homeownership rate in Switzerland is only around 40%, one of the lowest in the OECD, meaning that investment in rental properties plays an especially prominent role – whether by private individuals, commercial property

Figure 12. **Growth in domestic mortgage lending**

Year-on-year % change

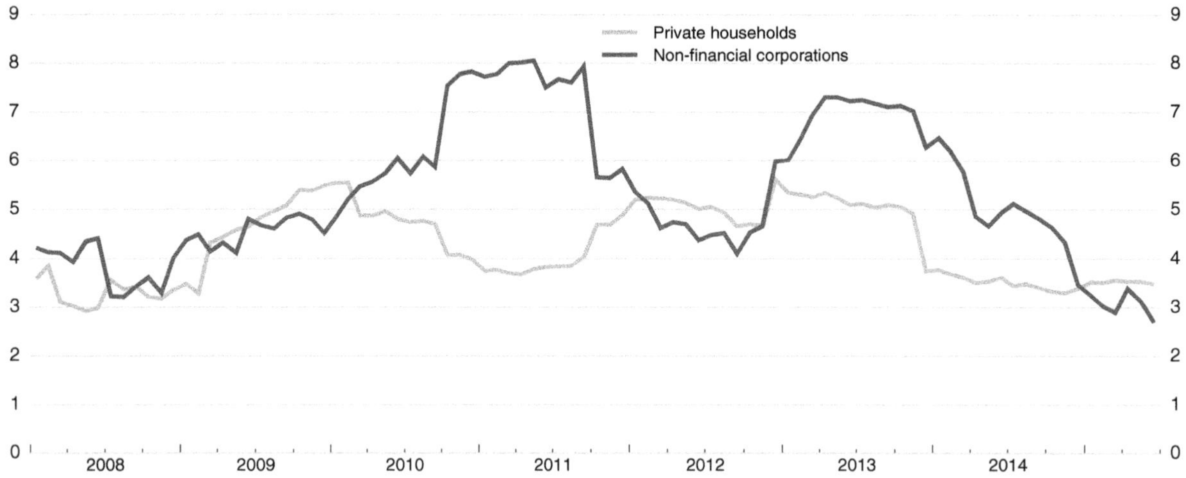

Source: Swiss National Bank, Monthly Statistical Bulletin and Monthly Bulletin of Banking Statistics, August 2015.

StatLink http://dx.doi.org/10.1787/888933292403

developers or institutional investors such as pension funds and insurance companies. Mortgage lending for the investment property segment should be monitored closely, as it may not be as responsive as households' borrowing to recent regulatory measures designed to rein it in (see below).

House price growth in Switzerland has been underpinned by strong immigration-driven population growth, shrinking household size (averaging 2.3 people in 2013, down from 3.4 in 1960), as well as unprecedentedly low mortgage interest rates, access to pension funds for pledges and down payments, and institutional and other private investors turning to real estate investment as yields on other asset classes have declined.

In Switzerland home owners are subject to a tax on imputed rental income, against which mortgage interest and other expenses such as maintenance and insurance costs are deductible. However there is a systematic undervaluation of imputed rent of up to 30-40% across the most populous cantons (Bourassa and Hoesli, 2010) and maintenance costs are frequently inflated so that in net households often claim a net tax deduction with regards to housing. The system would be made fairer if imputed rent calculations were calculated more frequently to better reflect market values and if limits were imposed on the tax deductibility of mortgage interest so that, combined with maintenance outlays, it does not exceed to the amount of declared imputed rent.

At the same time, the supply of housing in Switzerland has failed to respond to the surge in prices. Andrews et al. (2011) found the supply response to price changes in Switzerland to be the lowest in their sample of 21 OECD countries. The reasons for this muted supply response include the stringency of planning and building regulations, as was discussed in the 2009 *Survey*. The revised Federal Law on Spatial Planning strongly promotes densification, especially in areas with above-average accessibility by public transport. Cantonal construction laws are currently being reviewed to address conflicts with planning regulations, including those that inhibit densification. Yet the technical capacity of smaller municipalities to administer planning regulation may be curbing activity. In the end it is the owner of the property who decides on such works, and owners may be unaware that there exists a potential for higher density on the property. The capacity for increased densities in existing zones and structures (inner development) should be re-examined, a programme of individual property audits that assess the potential for added-value densification instituted and this information provided to property owners.

Managing risks from the housing market

Switzerland's prudential regulation of its mortgage lenders is a combination of self-regulation by the banks (often under pressure from the authorities) and legal directives. Self-regulation is harmonised across institutions by Swiss Bankers Association (SBA) guidelines, which are approved by the Swiss Financial Market Supervisory Authority (FINMA). In the domain of mortgage financing, SBA guidelines stipulate general rules as well as minimum standards, which are reinforced by legal directives laid down in the Capital Adequacy Ordinance (CAO). Based on the general rules, banks define their internal policies. For instance, internal policies contain guidelines for mortgage lending including that the loan-to-value ratio (LTV) should be around 80% for owner-occupied housing. Current SBA guidelines also cover valuation standards and calculation of a level of sustainable income, while banks' internal policies set the interest rate used in imputing interest payments (SBA, 2014). Nevertheless, LTVs exceed 80% in one in six new mortgages (Figure 13, Panel A).

Figure 13. **Share of new mortgages with high loan-to-value and implied debt-service-to-income ratios**

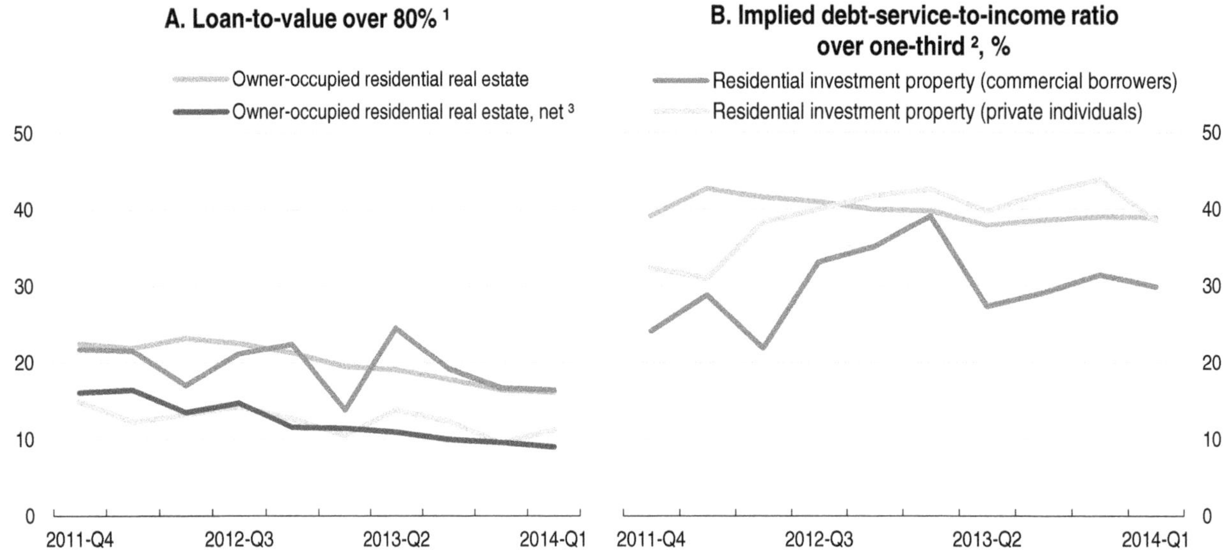

1. Proportion of new mortgages with LTVs above 80%.
2. Proportion of new mortgages with LTIs where imputed costs would exceed one-third of gross wage or pension income (private properties) or rental income (investment properties), respectively, at an interest rate of 5% as well as 1% for maintenance costs and 1% for amortisation costs.
3. Net figures including pledges from pillar 2 and 3a pension funds.

Source: SNB (2014), *Financial Stability Report 2014*, Zurich.

StatLink http://dx.doi.org/10.1787/888933292418

While recent self-regulation has concentrated on appropriate LTV ratios, affordability (debt service coverage) is equally if not more important. Banks are free, within the SBA guideline, to set their own policy in this regard. In calculating the debt service coverage, the use of a reference interest rate of 5% is commonly set by internal bank policy, with an additional 1% for maintenance costs and 1% for amortisation costs. Banks typically require that debt service payments not exceed one-third of household gross income. However, they often use a reference interest rate below 5% and are also flexible in other aspects such as which components of household income are included in affordability measures. The SNB survey indicates that in 2014 more than 40% of new mortgages for owner-occupied residences exceeded the one-third debt-service-to-income ratio threshold when applying a 5% interest rate (Figure 13, Panel B).

As to legal directives, a number of measures have been taken by the banks and authorities over the past three years to shore up banks' exposure and to take the heat out of the market. These include minimum standards implemented by SBA guidelines and reinforced by legal directives requiring that down payments comprise at least 10% of the purchase price from a borrower's own funds, and not include pledges or early withdrawals from the second pension pillar. Also, since 2014 amortisation must reach an LTV of two-thirds within 15 years. A counter-cyclical buffer (CCB) was activated at the beginning of 2013, which obliges banks to hold additional common equity Tier 1 capital based on their risk-weighted positions secured by residential real estate in Switzerland. In January 2014 the CCB was increased from 1% to 2%.

While there are signs of cooling, particularly in hotspots like Geneva and Zurich, house prices remain high and the risk to the banking sector elevated. In the light of this, the current range of policy measures should be given time to work. Moreover, the SNB and other regulators should maintain their communications strategy of warning households and investors of the growing risks of borrowing to purchase real estate. However, given the importance of affordability in terms of the exposure of the banking sector to a correction in the housing sector, consideration should be given to establishing a legal framework for explicitly addressing affordability risk, to be used if needed to contain financial stability risks related to imbalances in the housing and mortgage markets.

Recommendations for managing the housing cycle

- Establish a framework for explicitly addressing affordability risk, to be used if needed to contain financial stability risks related to imbalances in the housing and mortgage markets.
- Monitor closely mortgage lending to firms or households for rental properties, which may not be as responsive as the owner-occupied segment to recent regulatory measures.
- Review spatial planning regulations to make it easier to build denser housing.
- Limit the tax deductibility of mortgage interest so that, combined with maintenance outlays, it does not exceed the amount of declared imputed rent. Update the imputed rent calculations more frequently to better reflect market values.

Raising efficiency in public spending

Switzerland scores highly in various public policy outcomes. For instance, it ranked fifth in the 2012 PISA mathematics evaluation and, at 82.9 years, enjoys the second highest life expectancy at birth in Europe (EUROSTAT, 2015). Switzerland also had the OECD's lowest ratio of administrative costs to net revenue collection in 2013 (OECD, 2015c). As the population grows and ages – Avenir Suisse (2013) has calculated that the ratio of workers to retirees will fall from 3.8 in 2010 to 2 by 2050 – the country is going to face rising demand for public services and, unless productivity trends improve, downward pressure on revenues. A heavy focus on the efficiency of public expenditure is therefore critical.

The efficiency of public expenditure can be assessed by benchmarking outcomes against inputs in a variety of countries. Such analysis shows that Swiss public spending is indeed effective but not efficient (see Chapter 2). For instance, Germany and Switzerland had about the same score in the 2012 PISA reading assessment, but Switzerland spent 21.4% more per student than Germany.

Making the education system more inclusive and responsive to changes in the labour market

In the OECD's PISA assessments, in most countries pupils who attended early childhood education and care for more than one year achieved significantly better reading outcomes (OECD, 2014c). Thus, raising enrolment in pre-primary education promises high returns. But, as illustrated in the previous *Survey*, Swiss childcare services are both expensive and in short supply. Cantons and municipalities should increase direct public spending on additional early childhood education and care facilities and copy successful childcare voucher systems like those in the Canton of Lucerne.

Fostering access to early childhood education and care may be especially important for native-born children of immigrants. A survey of parents conducted in Basel and its environs showed that children with a migration background have the least opportunity to access facilities provided outside the family, thereby hampering their ability to master an official language early (CSRE, 2014). OECD research suggests that, despite improvements, immigration remains a risk factor for low academic performance which may have long-lasting consequences for individuals as they leave school and enter post-secondary education, training or the labour market (OECD 2012b; OECD, 2015d). At the same time, evidence shows that almost three quarters of the immigrants' under performance at school are to be accounted for by socio-economic determinants (Cattaneo and Wolter, 2015). Recent research also suggests that Switzerland performs relatively well regarding educational achievements of second-generation immigrants (Kunz, 2014).

At around 30%, university dropout rates are high (OECD, 2010b). In particular, baccalaureate graduates from certain cantons are overrepresented in university dropouts across Switzerland, suggesting that the quality of a baccalaureate is lower in these cantons. The impact of the baccalaureate rate in the canton of origin has indeed been shown to significantly increase the risk of dropping out (Wolter et al., 2014). In addition to being unfair and inefficient, this imposes additional costs on the other cantons, which finance the universities, and the Confederation, which funds institutes of technology. One way to address this problem is to set up a bonus-penalty system to encourage such cantons to reduce the number of university dropouts. Another option would be to increase resources for guidance counselling for high school students, in particular with regards to field-of-study choices. The dropout rates are particularly high among some foreign students who pay very low tuition fees by international comparison.

Another trend, although not specific to Switzerland, is the growing demand on the labour market for graduates trained in certain fields including science engineering, health care, and teaching. That demand is not being met by Switzerland's below-average share of tertiary type-A graduates (especially women) in STEM subjects. At the same time, because in many cases (such as health) similar qualifications can be obtained both from professional education and training, which does not require an academic or vocational baccalaureate for regular admission, and universities of applied sciences (UAS), about 30% of employed UAS graduates were in jobs not requiring a university degree. The government should look closely at labour market changes, the skills in need and job mismatches, and this information should be communicated to prospective students including through high school counselling.

Fostering value-based competition and better governance in health care

The Federal Law on Health Insurance requires Swiss residents to purchase basic health insurance, which insurers are required to offer to everyone, regardless of age or medical condition. In the Swiss health system, the cantons are accountable for guaranteeing access to medical services and monitoring that individuals hold basic health insurance. They also take care of disease prevention and health education. Municipalities do what is delegated by cantons, for example providing nursing and home care. As for the Confederation, it is responsible mostly for the regulation of health insurance.

Switzerland's excellent health-care system comes at a price. In 2012 it had the OECD's highest health-care spending per capita in PPP terms. Data envelopment analysis also shows that it is in the bottom quartile of health-care expenditure efficiency (Chapter 2). Some of this inefficiency stems from excessive fragmentation in the health-care system's structure and governance. It is estimated that, at around CHF 3 billion per year, inadequate co-ordination due to poor governance is the largest of all the system's inefficiency costs (SAAS, 2012). In the absence of a single-payer system, fragmentation in funding is also an issue. As the Swiss people rejected a single-payer public health insurance system by referendum in 2014, improvements will have to be made to the system as it currently operates.

A by-product of the system's fragmentation is an over-supply of health-care services. For instance, a comparatively large number of hospital beds has led to greater use of in-patient services. There are too many regional hospitals that tend to conduct too few operations to be cost effective and up to date with modern treatments and technology. For instance, there are 120 hospitals conducting vascular surgery in Switzerland, versus 8 in the whole of London (*La Tribune de Genève,* 2015). A reduction in their number should be encouraged. Inducing the insured to seek care within a restricted network of providers in exchange for lower insurance premiums ("managed care") would likewise raise efficiency. In any case, over-consultation can be mitigated by "gatekeeping", i.e. requiring patients to be referred by generalists in order to access specialists or hospitals.

Consumers often have little information about the quality of health-care providers in order to better inform their choices. Similarly, health professionals lack registries publishing the results of specialised treatments. Switzerland would benefit from systematic data collection across the full spectrum of health-care services. Besides the quality indicators published by the Federal Office of Public Health, an organisation called the *Association nationale pour le développement de la qualité dans les hôpitaux et les cliniques* (ANQ) is now responsible for co-ordinating and producing quality indicators at hospitals and clinics. A set of quality indicators for primary care and outpatient activity is still lacking, however.

A dearth of data also hinders the assessment of appropriate base rates charged by hospitals. The payment per case is calculated by multiplying the so-called base rate (which is agreed between insurers and hospitals and approved by cantonal governments) by a coefficient (which is disease-specific yet uniform at the national level). Differences in treatment costs across hospitals are taken into account in the negotiation. If no agreement is reached, administrative tribunals settle the dispute. They recently validated base rates of CHF 10325 in Lucerne, significantly more than the recommended base rate of CHF 8 974 calculated based on exploratory benchmarking in the cantons of Zurich and Thurgovie (Confédération Suisse, 2014). Costs per case rose by 2.5% in 2013 (Interpharma, 2015). More and better information via registries and systematic cost-effectiveness analysis would help benchmark costs per procedure and limit the rise in spending. If rulings by administrative tribunals do not succeed in limiting the upward pressure on base rates, new regulation may be needed to circumscribe the ability of hospitals and insurers to set base rates.

Drugs, which accounted for 9.2% of total health-care costs in 2012, tend to be relatively expensive in Switzerland. Due to the rule for setting their prices, generics in particular are on average nearly three times as expensive as in neighbouring countries. That rule requires that generics be priced, depending on sales volume, at least 10 to 60% below the price of the original patented medicine at the time of its patent expiry. In addition, health insurance reimburses both the generic and the original drug, thereby decreasing the incentive to choose the generic, resulting in overconsumption of branded drugs and a low share of generics by value in international comparison (Figure 14). In order to force prices down, reimbursement should be set to a pre-determined fixed amount, as is done in more than

20 other European countries (Confédération Suisse, 2014). According to Santésuisse (an association of insurers), such measures could save CHF 125 per patient per year, which is CHF 1 billion overall. Reviewing drug prices at least every year (rather than every three years) to better reflect exchange rates would also help.

Figure 14. **Share of generics in the total pharmaceutical market, 2013 (or nearest year)**

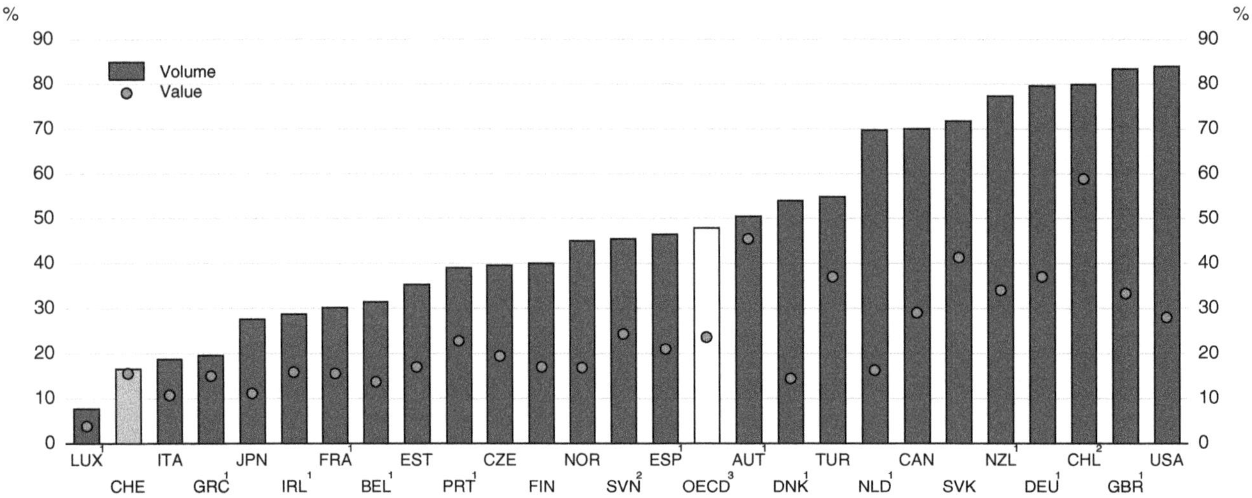

1. Reimbursed pharmaceutical market.
2. Community pharmacy market.
3. Simple average of the 26 countries with available data.

Source: OECD, *Health at a Glance 2015*.

StatLink http://dx.doi.org/10.1787/888933292422

Transport infrastructure is also a good candidate for raising spending efficiency

At recent trends the annual cost of Swiss traffic congestion is estimated to have reached CHF 1 billion, three times as much as in 2000 (OFR, 2013). More efficient use of transport infrastructure would, over the long term, reduce the need to invest in more of it. Congestion could be reduced by charging a higher price at peak traffic times, a system known as peak-load pricing. Electronic tolling station or satellite-based registration could be used for roads and time-based pricing further built into rail transportation. To avoid undesired substitution effects, a comprehensive approach should be adopted. Only once such a pricing system is in place can policymakers see clearly when true infrastructure shortages justify greater investment spending.

Broadening the use of public tendering

More tendering of public contracts can also boost the efficiency of public spending. Despite liberalisation of the system in the 1990s and the launch of a centralising web-based platform in 2009, outside procurement as a percentage of public spending (23%) is still below the OECD average of 29% (OECD, 2013d). About 20% is carried out by the federal, 35% by the cantonal and 45% by municipal governments. Potential for improving efficiency remains high due to a lack of homogeneity in procedures. A revision of legal frameworks is currently underway and includes an alignment of cantonal and federal legislation with the revised WTO General Procurement Agreement, which came into force in April 2014. This should lead to greater standardisation in procedures and foster fair and transparent competition. Switzerland should implement standardised procedures across all of its jurisdictions.

Addressing rising welfare expenditure

While federal and cantonal debts are back to acceptable levels, the outlook for social security spending is increasingly beholden to demographic forces. The number of workers per pensioner fell from 6.2 in 1950 to 3.8 in 2010. Depending on cost containment scenarios, public health and long-term care expenditures are projected to increase between 1.9 and 2.6 percentage points of GDP by 2030 from about 7% of GDP today (Figure 15). If the 1990-2007 growth rates for social and health-care spending were to continue, they would absorb 70% of all public expenditure in 2030, versus 38% today (économiesuisse, 2012). Such spending risks crowding out other important expenditures.

Figure 15. **Public expenditure on health care is set to increase in the medium term**

As a percentage of GDP

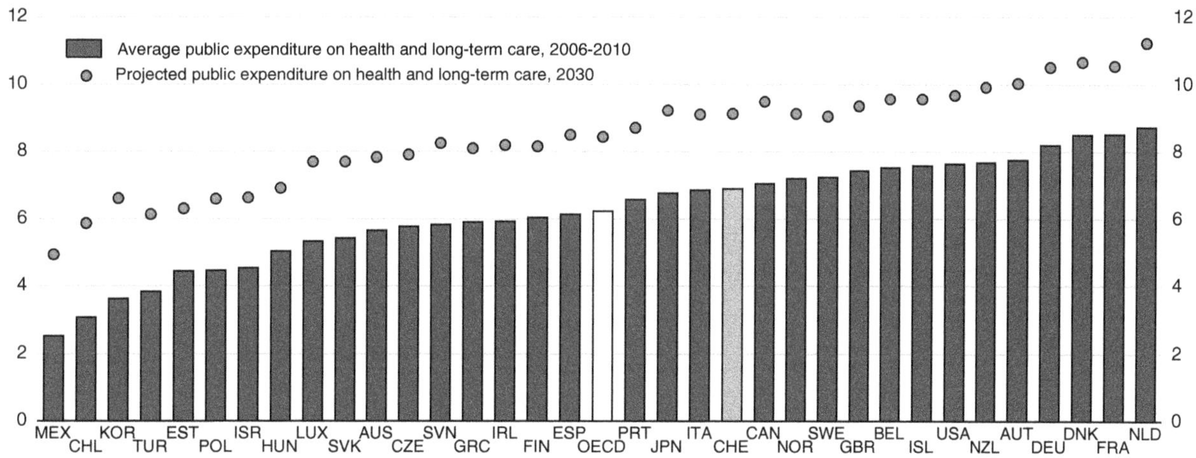

Source: De la Maisonneuve, C. and J. Oliveira Martins (2013), "A Projection Method for Public Health and Long-Term Care Expenditures", *OECD Economics Department Working Papers*, No. 1048, OECD Publishing.

StatLink *http://dx.doi.org/10.1787/888933292439*

In a comprehensive assessment of social security reform, Keuschnigg et al. (2011) find that increasing the retirement age is the most effective means of limiting the negative impact of aging on economic growth and fiscal sustainability. A rise in the VAT came second in terms of effectiveness. A comprehensive pension reform (Prévoyance Vieillesse 2020) is currently being discussed in Parliament. The main proposals are a harmonisation of the retirement age at 65 years, currently 64 for women), an increase in the VAT rate by 1.5 percentage points to fund the first pillar, more flexibility in the transition to retirement, and a decrease from 6.8 to 6% in the rate of return on retirement savings accumulated in the second pillar (the "conversion rate").

Another option is to boost labour supply of older workers by paying higher pensions to people who have worked beyond the normal retirement age. For instance, pensions are raised by 12% in Portugal for every year of additional work, 10.4% in the United Kingdom and 8.4% in Japan. In Switzerland pensions go up only between 5.2% and 6.3% (OECD, 2013a). Incentives for early retirement, especially in the second pillar, ranging from mandatory early retirement to very attractive packages for the most successful employees, should be reduced (OECD, 2014d). In Switzerland, only 665 companies (slightly above 1%) employ staff who are beyond the legal retirement age (*Le Temps*, 2015). Also, on-the-job training for people aged 55-64 without a university degree is seven times lower than for workers with a degree. Targeted programmes should be developed to raise the skills of older workers without degrees.

Improving fiscal equalisation

Switzerland has a system of fiscal equalisation that uses financial transfers across heterogeneous cantons (totalling CHF 4.5 billion or 0.7% of GDP in 2014) to provide minimum acceptable levels of public services across all cantons. It has two main components: resource equalisation and cost compensation, and there is also a cohesion fund, totalling CHF 366 million, to cushion the effect of recent reforms. Because some cantons have greater revenue potential than others, resource equalisation aims at levelling the playing field in terms of attracting residents and businesses by, for instance, allowing lower-revenue-potential cantons to offer competitive tax rates. However, the current system creates little incentive for less wealthy cantons to raise their resource potential: the equalisation framework operates so that cantons face a corresponding decrease in fiscal transfers, on average equal to 80% of the revenue raised (Conseil Fédéral, 2014). The implicit marginal tax rate of 80% should be reduced. In parallel, putting a smaller weight on firm profits in the calculation of resource potential should foster attractiveness while limiting the rise in revenue potential, as discussed in Corporate Tax Reform III. Cost compensation, by contrast, aims at offsetting higher public service costs due to geographic or demographic features. But the current 50-50 allocation between socio-demographic and topographic factors is detrimental to cities and should be revised by raising the percentage dedicated to the former.

Recommendations for increasing public spending efficiency and improving the fiscal framework

Key recommendations

- Increase public spending on early childhood education and care, especially for children with disadvantaged socio-economic backgrounds (including those from immigrant backgrounds), which could be combined with a generalisation of the childcare voucher system in the Canton of Lucerne.
- Evaluate solutions to reduce the drop-out rate in the university system.
- Boost the supply and attractiveness of fields of study that are in high demand in the labour market. Further clarify study streams across the tertiary education system.
- Switch the system for setting generic drug prices to reimbursing a pre-determined fixed amount.
- Encourage systematic benchmarking of hospital costs. If rates keep rising despite recent reforms, consider new legislation to control them using cost benchmarks.
- Fix the retirement age at 65 for both sexes and thereafter link it to life expectancy. To cut early retirement, reduce existing incentives and pay a larger pension premium for those who choose to work longer.

Other recommendations

- Increase the share of public expenditure allocated via tenders, and harmonise procurement procedures across all levels of government.
- Create incentives for people to join managed-care networks.

Adjusting to international best practice on tax issues, including information exchange

Cantonal tax regimes and ring fencing

For decades special cantonal tax regimes have existed for resident companies that carry on only limited commercial activities within Switzerland, so income of such companies from foreign sources is taxed less than Swiss-source income. Since the entry into force of the 1990 Federal Act on the Harmonization of the Cantonal and Municipal Income Taxes, the cantonal rules applicable to these companies have been harmonised.

In line with Switzerland's commitment to the OECD-G20 Base Erosion and Profit Shifting (BEPS) Project, which commenced in 2013, and the joint declaration between Switzerland and the EU signed in October 2014, Switzerland undertook to amend the relevant features of its corporate tax system. The resulting Corporate Tax Reform III package, proposed by the Federal Council to parliament, is a comprehensive set of measures aiming to ensure alignment with the international tax rules, to provide for a competitive tax environment and to ensure the flow of corporate revenues. These aims are to be reached by different measures, such as:

- The existing regimes are to be discontinued. Thus, cantonal tax status as well as administrative practices concerning principal companies and Swiss finance branches will be abrogated.
- A patent box on cantonal level in line with the principles on preferential tax regimes agreed in the OECD – G20 BEPS Project is to be introduced. Additionally, the cantons may implement super-deductions for research and development (R&D) expenditure. While the patent box provides support for the output of the R&D process, the super-deduction for R&D expenditures provide for support for R&D inputs by allowing a deduction of more than 100% of this expenditure.
- Cuts in corporate income tax rates are within each canton's sovereignty.
- The Confederation will support the cantons by increasing their share of federal corporate tax revenues from 17 per cent to 20.5 per cent and an adjustment of the system of financial equalisation.

The reform is expected to be completed by 2017-19 or later, in case of a referendum.

The OECD's Base Erosion and Profit Shifting (BEPS) initiative

International tax arrangements have come under intense scrutiny since the financial crisis. The OECD-G20 BEPS Project undertook to review the international tax system to ensure that the rules align taxation of profits with underlying economic activity and value creation, and increase transparency. Switzerland is popular as a location for registering business intangibles, such as patents, property rights and brands (OECD, 2013c). For this reason, its active engagement in the development of the measures to counter profit shifting is very welcome, as is its adherence to the 2013 Declaration on Base Erosion and Profit Shifting, which recognises the pressing need to address the asymmetries in domestic and international tax rules, and work towards a level-playing field in this area.

The OECD BEPS Action Plan consists of 15 Actions aimed at revising the international tax rules to address the mismatches and loopholes that allow the location of profits to be separated from the underlying economic activity and value creation, which often results in little or no corporate income tax paid by multinational firms (OECD, 2013a). The first seven deliverables were published in September 2014 and the final reports regarding all actions are to be published in October 2015. The full package of BEPS measures will be finalised at the end of September, and Switzerland should continue to play an active role in working towards a consensus agreement on the package of measures. Looking ahead, it will be important for all countries, including Switzerland, to work quickly to implement the measures agreed to ensure a level playing field. As part of those efforts, Switzerland has recently agreed to participate in the ad hoc group for the negotiation of the multilateral instrument (Action 15 of the BEPS Action Plan), which will allow countries to quickly implement the tax-treaty-related BEPS measures in their existing networks of bilateral tax treaties.

Implementing international standards regarding exchange of information in tax matters

Exchange of information on request

The Global Forum on Transparency and Exchange of Information for Tax Purposes monitors the effective implementation of the internationally agreed standard for the exchange of information (EOI) on request where it is foreseeably relevant to the administration and enforcement of the domestic tax laws of the requesting jurisdiction. Through a two-phase Peer Review process, it assesses compliance with that standard and publishes its reports and overall ratings. Switzerland is an active member of the Global Forum; it is a member of its Steering Group, Peer Review Group and Automatic Exchange of Information Group.

In March 2009, Switzerland committed to the international standard and withdrew its reservation to Article 26 of the OECD Model Tax Convention. The Global Forum's Phase 1 review of Switzerland was finalised and published in 2011. The Phase 1 report concluded that in a number of significant regards, including access to bank information, Switzerland's legal and regulatory framework did not meet the EOI standard. The Phase 1 report concluded that progress to Phase 2 should be conditional on improvements of its legal and regulatory framework, improvements that needed to be evaluated in a supplementary review.

Following changes made to its legal and regulatory framework, Switzerland's request for a Supplementary review was accepted, and it was launched in July 2014. The ensuing report, which was published in March 2015, concluded that Switzerland had met the conditions to progress to Phase 2 review. Switzerland's Phase 2 review will be launched in the fourth quarter of 2015 and is expected to be published by mid-2016. This Phase 2 review will assess Switzerland's implementation of the EOI standard in practice. At that stage, Switzerland will be assigned an overall compliancy rating by the Global Forum.

The Global Forum is also currently involved in a review of its Terms of Reference. The changes will include the requirement for jurisdictions to ensure the availability of beneficial ownership information in line with FATF requirements. All Global Forum member jurisdictions will be reviewed for compliance with the updated Terms of Reference in a second round of reviews during the period 2016-20.

Automatic exchange of information

Alongside the international framework for the EOI on request, in September 2013 the G20 endorsed the OECD proposal for a global Standard for Automatic Exchange of Financial Account Information in Tax Matters (AEOI). This Standard, which was approved by the OECD in July 2014, requires jurisdictions to automatically exchange financial account information with other jurisdictions on an annual basis. The AEOI Standard sets out the financial institutions required to report such information, the account information to be exchanged, the different types of accounts and taxpayers covered, as well as common due diligence procedures to be followed by these institutions. Importantly, unlike EOI on request, AEOI data is transmitted without recipient countries having to send a specific request.

Switzerland has committed to implementing the new AEOI standard and making the first exchanges under AEOI by September 2018, and is working to pass the necessary laws and put in place the other necessary implementation measures. In November 2014, Switzerland became the 52nd jurisdiction to sign the Multilateral Competent Authority Agreement (MCAA), which is an important tool that will assist Switzerland in undertaking AEOI with its partners. In May 2015, it entered into an agreement with the EU for the automatic exchange of information in accordance with the Standard. In June 2015 the Swiss Federal Council submitted draft implementing legislation to Parliament that also includes legislation to ratify the MCAA and the multilateral Convention for Mutual Administrative Assistance in Tax Matters (the Convention). The Parliament is expected to begin deliberations on the proposed legislation in autumn 2015. The legislative process provides for the possibility of a referendum. By giving effect to the Convention and the MCAA, which are international instruments in which all jurisdictions can participate, Switzerland will be able to exchange financial account information on an automatic basis with a wide range of partner jurisdictions.

Recommendations on international tax issues and information sharing

- Follow the recommendations and participate in the implementation and post-2015 follow-up of the OECD-G20 BEPS Project.
- Address the recommendations made by the Global Forum on Transparency and Exchange of Information for Tax Purposes, and ensure compliance with the Exchange of Information on request standard.
- Prioritise the legislative implementation of automatic exchange of information.

Bibliography

Andrews, D., A. Caldera Sánchez and Å. Johansson (2011), "Housing Markets and Structural Policies in OECD Countries", *OECD Economics Department Working Papers*, No. 836, OECD Publishing.

Auer, R and P. Sauré (2011), "Export Basket and the Effects of Exchange Rates on Exports – Why Switzerland is Special", Federal Reserve Bank of Dallas Globalization and Monetary Policy Institute, *Working Paper*, No. 77.

Avenir Suisse (2013), *Une cure de jouvence pour la prévoyance vieillesse : Propositions de réforme du deuxième pilier*, Zurich.

Bloomberg (2015), "Franc Surge Supercharges Swiss Spending Power in German Towns", 27 April.

Bourassa, S. and M. Hoesli (2010), "Why Do the Swiss Rent?", *Journal of Real Estate Finance and Economics*, Vol. 40, No. 3, pp. 286-309.

Cattaneo, M. and S. Wolter (2015),"Better Migrants: better PISA Results. Findings from a Natural Experiment", *IZA Journal of Migration*, forthcoming.

Confédération Suisse (2014), *Rapport annuel du surveillant des prix*, Bern.

Conseil Fédéral (2014), *Rapport sur l'évaluation de l'efficacité 2012-15 de la péréquation financière entre la Confédération et les cantons*, Bern.

CSRE (2014), *Swiss Education Report 2014*, Centre suisse de coordination pour la recherche en éducation, Aarau.

Demmou, L., M. Haluš, G. Machlica and F. Menkyna (2015), "Spurring Growth in Lagging Regions in the Slovak Republic", *OECD Economics Department Working Papers*, No. 1211, OECD Publishing.

économiesuisse (2012), *Garantir la pérennité des assurances sociales grâce à des mécanismes d'intervention*, dossier politique No. 19, Geneva.

EUROSTAT (2015), Mortality and life expectancy statistic, Kirchberg, Luxembourg.

FEDRO (2013), *Trafic et disponibilité des routes nationales, Rapport annuel 2013*, Federal roads office, Bern.

FSO (2014), "Environment Pocket Statistics 2014", Federal statistical office, Neuchâtel.

Interpharma (2015), *Santé Publique en Suisse*, Basel.

Keuschnigg, C., M. Keuschnigg and C. Jaag (2011), "Aging and the Financing of Social Security in Switzerland", *Swiss Journal of Economics and Statistics*, Vol. 147, No. 2, pp. 181-231.

KOF (2015a), "KOF employment indicator: increase in the value of the franc is making itself felt on the labour market", *KOF Bulletin*, No. 85, May, Business cycle research center of EPF Zurich.

KOF (2015b), "The Swiss franc exchange rate shock and Swiss foreign trade in the first quarter 2015", *KOF Bulletin*, No. 85, May, Business cycle research center of EPF Zurich.

Kunz, J. (2014), "Analyzing Educational Achivement Differences Between Second-Generation Immigrants: Comparing Germany and German-speaking Switzerland", *CESifo Working Paper* No. 5020, Munich.

La Tribune de Genève (2015), "Le réformateur des hôpitaux suisses était genevois", 29 May.

Le Temps (2015), "Avenir Suisse défend la flexibilité des retraites", 28 January.

LINK Institute (2014), *Baromètre des places d'apprentissage*, Rapport détaillé, August.

Moody's (2012), "Credit Opinion: Swisscom AG", Moody's Investor Service Global Credit Research, April.

Müller, B. and J. Schweri (2012), "Die Betriebe in der dualen Berufsbildung: Entwicklungen 1985 bis 2008", Bureau of federal statistics, Neuchâtel.

OECD (2010a), *Sickness, Disability and Work: Breaking the Barriers*, OECD Publishing.

OECD (2010b), *Education at a Glance 2010*, OECD Publishing.

OECD (2012a), *OECD Economic Survey of Switzerland 2012*, OECD Publishing.

OECD (2012b), *Untapped Skills: Realizing the potential of immigrant students*, OECD Publishing.

OECD (2013a), *Addressing Base Erosion and Profit Shifting*, OECD Publishing, *http://dx.doi.org/10.1787/9789264192744-en*.

OECD (2013b), *OECD Communications Outlook 2013*, OECD Publishing, *www.oecd.org/sti/broadband/oecd-communications-outlook-19991460.htm*.

OECD (2013c), *OECD Economic Survey of Switzerland 2013*, OECD Publishing.

OECD (2013d), *Government at a Glance 2013*, OECD Publishing.

OECD (2014a), *OECD Economic Surveys: Germany 2014*, OECD Publishing.

OECD (2014b), *International Migration Outlook 2014*, OECD Publishing.

OECD (2014c), "Does pre-primary education reach those who need it most?", *PISA in Focus*, Vol.40, OECD Publishing.

OECD (2014d), *Vieillissement et politiques de l'emploi, Suisse – Mieux travailler avec l'âge*, OECD Publishing.

OECD (2015a), *OECD Economic Outlook 97*, June, OECD Publishing.

OECD (2015b), *The Future of Productivity*, July, OECD Publishing.

OECD (2015c), *Government at a Glance 2015*, OECD Publishing.

OECD (2015d), "Can the performance gap between immigrant and non-immigrant students be closed?", *PISA in Focus*, Vol. 53, OECD Publishing.

SAAS (2012), *Effizienz, Nutzung und Finanzierung des Gesundheitswesens*, Swiss Academy of Arts and Sciences, Bern.

SBA (2014), "Richtlinien für die Prüfung, Bewertung und Abwicklung grundpfandgesicherter Kredite", Swiss Bankers Association, Basel.

Schaltegger, C., R. Hofmann and Z. Huwyler (2015), "La péréquation financière au banc de la pratique: l'exemple de Bâle-Campagne", *La Vie Économique*, 1-2/2015, pp. 41-45.

SECO (2015), *Principes pour une nouvelle politique de croissance*, State secretariat for economic affairs, Bern.

SFOE and SFOH (2015), "Energetische Sanierung Auswirkungen auf Mietzinsen: Schlussbericht", Swiss Federal Office of Energy and Swiss Federal Office of Housing.

SNB (2014), "Implementing the countercyclical capital buffer in Switzerland: concretising the Swiss National Bank's role", Swiss National Bank, Bern-Zurich.

SNB (2015), *Financial Stability Report 2015*, Swiss National Bank, Zurich.

Standard and Poor's (2015), "Swisscom AG", Standard and Poor's Ratings Services, McGraw Hill Financial, May 2015.

Sung, N. (2014), "Market concentration and competition in OECD mobile telecommunications markets", *Applied Economics*, Vol. 46, Issue 25, pp. 3037-48, September, *http://dx.doi.org/10.1080/00036846.2014.920480*.

Swisscom (2014), *2014 Annual Report*, Bern, *www.swisscom.ch/content/dam/swisscom/de/about/investoren/documents/2015/2014-annual-results.pdf*.

Wölfl, A. and P. Sicari (2012), "Reducing Greenhouse Gas Emissions in a Cost Effective Way in Switzerland", *OECD Economics Department Working Papers*, No. 1002, OECD Publishing, *http://dx.doi.org/10.1787/5k8xff3tgd32-en*.

Wolter, S., A. Diem and D. Messer (2014), "Drop-outs from Swiss Universities: an empirical analysis of data on all students between 1975 and 2008", *European Journal of Education*, Vol. 49, Issue 4, pp. 471-483.

WTO (2013), *Trade Policy Review, Review by the Secretariat: Switzerland and Liechtenstein*, WT/TPR/S/280, 19 March.

WTO (2014), *Trade Policy Review, Review by the Secretariat: The United States*, WT/TPR/S/307, 11 November.

WTO (2015), *Trade Policy Review, Review by the Secretariat: Australia*, WT/TPR/S/312, 3 March.

ANNEX

Progress in structural reform

This table reviews action taken on recommendations from previous Surveys. Recommendations that are new in this Survey are listed at the end of the relevant chapter.

Recommendations in previous *Surveys*	Action taken since September 2013
A. Boosting long term growth and productivity	
Examine the roots of, and propose remedies for the poor productivity performance, including by creating a productivity commission.	A report entitled "Principles for a New Growth Policy" was published in January 2015.
Accelerate the pace of agricultural sector reform, including moving entirely to direct payments to farmers, and by further integrating the entire food value chain in international trade.	In December 2014 a project was launched to simplify the administration of agricultural policy and current regulations. Results are expected by December 2015.
Redouble efforts to negotiate FTAs, especially with economically important economies.	An FTA with China and the Gulf Co-operation Council entered into force on 1 July 2014, with the Central American States on 29 August 2014 and with Bosnia-Herzegovina on 1 January 2015. Negotiations are underway with the Philippines and Georgia and are continuing with Malaysia and Vietnam. Negotiations are stalled with India, Indonesia and Russia/Belarus/ Kazakhstan. Negotiations with Turkey to modernise and broaden the scope of the existing agreement have started.
Continue to examine options for the introduction of tax incentives that encourage innovation, for example for business angels.	No action taken.
Be prudent with the tax treatment of intellectual property to ensure that current measures are serving their intended purpose and are not unduly distortionary internationally.	A corporate tax reform proposed by the Federal Council to the parliament in June 2015 includes the introduction of a "patent box" under which income from intellectual property such as patents will be eligible for preferential tax treatment in line with the emerging OECD standard.
Ease restrictions on starting a business by reducing the number of procedures and time required, for example by improving the web-portal "StartBiz" and abolishing the compulsory public notary authentication.	It has been possible to create a public company fully electronically since April 2015. Previously, this was limited to private companies (sole proprietorship).
Put more emphasis on the early labour market activation of migrants.	Since January 2014 the Confederation and cantons have been working together to improve integration. Cantons, in collaboration with the Confederation, have developed cantonal integration programs within three fields of promotion: information and counselling, education and employment, mutual understanding and social integration. The early labour market activation of migrants is an important aim of these programs.
Give a more important role to job-insertion allowances, which provide subsidies to companies to employ young, inexperienced or the long-term unemployed.	Expenses for job-insertion allowances have risen from about CHF 11 to 23 million between 2011 and 2014.
Do more at the federal level to co-ordinate employment services between cantons.	No action taken.
B. Upgrading education	
Step up public funding of pre-schools.	Federal financial support has been extended until 2019.
Address integration issues within the integrated school system as part of a comprehensive policy.	Since January 2014 each canton has adopted an integration programme, bundling all specific measures for fostering integration into a comprehensive policy. Two out of eight strategic domains deal with education (language education and early childhood education).
Learn from the experience of other countries, including Finland, with their teacher preparation programmes, which focus intensively on helping teachers develop practical remedial teaching skills that help to address weaker students within aptitude-level integrated classrooms.	No action taken.
Monitor closely the effects of delayed tracking on education outcomes.	A systematic monitoring of the education system has been in place since 2010.
Review the vocational and academic educational streams, especially in light of vacancies in some high-skill occupations and the reliance on immigrants to fill these positions.	No action taken.
Improve access to tertiary education for all segments of society, including special measures for those from lower socio-economic and immigrant backgrounds.	An inter-cantonal agreement on the harmonization of scholarships for upper secondary and tertiary education has been in place since 2013.

Recommendations in previous *Surveys*	Action taken since September 2013
C. Enhancing competition	
Consider allowing criminal sanctions for anti-competitive actions.	No action taken.
Apply the prohibition principle to all hard-core cartels. Raise ComCo's resources and ensure its independence by excluding members that represent economic interests.	No action taken.
In the electricity sector, introduce ownership separation between generation and transmission; strengthen the regulator's powers; introduce price caps and benchmark regulation; use regulatory accounting rules for the determination of network access prices.	Operational separation of the Swiss transmission system operator Swiss Grid from other activities is in force since 3 January 2013.
In telecommunications, apply ex ante regulation to access conditions to the local loop and to interconnection charges.	No action taken.
Make tendering of regional rail passenger services compulsory, ensure non-discriminatory access to rolling stock, and allow PKP's rivals to propose investment projects. Base investment decisions on an independent cost-benefit assessment.	No action taken.
Liberalise completely network industries, benchmark the public sector, and implement more efficient territorial management.	Regarding territorial management, the first step of the Spatial Planning Act's revision came into force in May 2014 and the cantons have 5 years to adapt their master plan accordingly (urbanization). Public consultation on the second step ended in May 2015 (protection of agricultural land, better co-ordination in the planning process of transport and energy infrastructures with territorial development, development of spatial cross-cantonal-border planning).
D. Improving the tax system	
Widen the VAT base by removing exemptions. Unify VAT rates. Over the medium term raise VAT rates. Explore the technical feasibility of applying a VAT to banking services. If such a VAT is not introduced, consider an additional tax on financial institutions' profits and remuneration.	No action taken.
Lower the tax wedge on second earners, for example, by introducing separate assessment of partner income. Set up uniform rules concerning the taxation of several earners within one household across levels of government.	No action taken.
Replace progressive cantonal corporate taxes with proportional taxes and abolish capital taxes. Remove taxes on the issuance of equity and debt securities.	The abolition of the issuance tax on equity is part of the Corporate Tax Reform III package proposed by the Federal Council to the parliament in June 2015.
Abolish the lump-sum tax regime for rich individuals who are not economically active in Switzerland. Subject all residents to standard personal income taxation.	The Swiss people rejected the popular initiative entitled "Stop the tax privileges for millionaires (abolition of lump-sum taxation)" on 30 November 2014.
E. Addressing environmental sustainability	
Put greater emphasis on market mechanisms in the transition from nuclear to renewable energy.	Partial reform of renewables support in 2014 replaced feed-in tariffs for rooftop photovoltaics with capital grants.
Implement a CO_2 levy on transport fuels.	No action taken.
Further promote private- and public-sector energy-related research, and continue engagement with foreign researchers to facilitate realisation of the Energy Strategy 2050.	Public energy R&D funding was stepped up 25% to CHF 250 million per annum in 2014.
Exploit the opportunities offered by the move from nuclear to renewable sources of energy and green-house gas targets to put in place a framework that promotes competition in the energy sector.	The Government plans to fully open the electricity market by decree. Full opening may, however, be challenged by referendum. A (partial) opening of the gas market is scheduled for around 2020.

Recommendations in previous *Surveys*	Action taken since September 2013
F. Expanding women's role in the economy	
Use role models to make hard sciences more attractive for girls and social sciences and health to boys, and raise awareness of career and earnings prospects associated with study choices. Inform students about rewarding gender-atypical career choices.	No action taken.
Facilitate greater mobility between career paths by creating well-marked and more numerous pathways.	No action taken.
Reduce the influence of socio-economic background on the extent of gender-typical study and career choices by providing earlier and more intensive guidance for disadvantaged students, and greater financial support.	No action taken.
Increase women's labour market options by raising public spending on childcare and by adjusting regulations to broaden the range of available price/quality options.	The Parliament decided in September 2014 to extend the Confederation's start-up funding for expanding supplementary childcare facilities from January 2015 until January 2019.
Remove the so-called marriage tax penalty at the federal level by introducing individual, as opposed to family, taxation or some equivalent measure.	No action taken.
Create paternity leave, and consecutive "take it or leave it" parental leave to be shared between fathers and mothers.	No action taken.
Introduce a time-limited entitlement to part-time work for parents with very young children.	Since 2013 federal employees have been allowed to reduce their working hours following the birth of a child.
Implement a corporate governance code establishing gender goals to increase the number of women in senior management.	A revised Code of Best Practice for Corporate Governance was completed on 29 September 2014, and a new article 12 on the representation of women was introduced.
Increase the proportion of women on company boards by setting ambitious targets combined with a "Comply or Explain" requirement or by setting quotas.	No action taken.
Foster a positive image of entrepreneurship amongst women by allowing successful women entrepreneurs to tour secondary and tertiary educational institutions to explain the rewards and advantages of setting up one's own business, especially given women's preference for flexible work solutions.	No action taken.
G. Reforming old-age and disability insurance programmes	
Index the retirement age in the first-pillar system to changes in average life expectancy. Deal with lack of sustainability through adjustments to contribution rates, benefits and required years of contributions.	A comprehensive pension reform (Prévoyance Vieillesse 2020) is currently before Parliament. The main changes are a harmonisation of the retirement age at 65 years (currently 64 for women), an increase in the VAT rate by 1.5 percentage points to fund the first pillar, more flexibility in the transition to retirement, and a decrease from 6.8 to 6% in the rate of return on retirement savings accumulated in the second pillar (the "conversion rate").
Introduce incentives for prolonging work after the standard retirement age.	According to the draft bill in Parliament, increased flexibility and individualization of the transition to retirement will be introduced. The insured will be able to choose the time of retirement from 62 to 70 years and between a full or partial pension. Contributions paid during that time will increase the postponed part of the pension. The maximum deferral period remains five years.
Allow pension funds to set the conversion rate.	None. This could violate the Constitution's social objective of a minimum benefit level.
Reassess the generosity of tax incentives for the occupational pension schemes.	Securing retirement income is a priority objective. With tax postponed until the pension (or the capital) is paid, there is a strong incentive to accrue retirement assets.
Cut the marginal effective tax rates on labour income of disability insurance beneficiaries. Regularly test their work capacities during the first few years of receipt and randomly thereafter.	The reassessment of invalidity benefit recipients introduced in 2012 is being evaluated (first results in December 2015, detailed results in the Outcome Reporting Project in 2019).

Recommendations in previous *Surveys*	Action taken since September 2013
H. Improving the regulation of Financial intermediaries	
Consider periodic rotation of the outside auditors responsible for particular financial institutions, and widen the range of authorised external auditors.	FINMA Circular 2013/3 provides the possibility to mandate experts that are not in charge of the ordinary audit to investigate a special field, and FINMA uses this option.
Complement the accounting triggers for the contingent convertible bonds (CoCos) by market indicators. FINMA could, for example, be required to request an independent audit of a bank's book value when market indicators drop below predefined values. A higher trigger of 7% of common equity relative to risk-weighted assets should be introduced for all CoCos.	No action taken.
Develop resolution plans for the large Swiss insurers.	No action taken.
Eliminate explicit cantonal government guarantees to their cantonal banks.	Currently most cantons retain a comprehensive guarantee for their cantonal banks, though for some it is limited. The Canton of Bern phased out its guarantee by 2013, and in 2011 the Canton of Geneva decided to completely phase out its currently limited guarantee by 2016.

Thematic chapters

Chapter 1

Policies to tame the housing cycle

Since 2000, real estate prices in Switzerland have risen rapidly. By some measures, between 2000 and 2014 apartment prices almost doubled, while those of single-family homes increased by around 60%. Price rises have varied considerably across cantons. Transactions activity in the sector has been robust, with growth in mortgage volumes strongly outpacing disposable income. As a consequence, Switzerland's residential mortgage debt-to-GDP ratio, at 120%, is the highest in the OECD. This is despite a private ownership rate of only around 40%, one of the lowest in the OECD. Banks' exposure to the mortgage market is the sixth highest in the OECD, with mortgages making up over 80% of domestic (non-interbank) bank loans. That said, high house prices are being supported by very low interest rates, immigration-fuelled population growth and smaller family units, while demand is being bolstered by mortgage interest tax deductibility and institutional investors. Restrictive planning regulations have also damped the supply response. These factors have contributed to low rental yields, although high compared to other assets and very low vacancy rates. A number of measures have been taken by banks and authorities over the past three years to shore up banks' exposure and to take the heat out of the market. These include a minimum down payment of 10% of the collateral value of the property from the borrower's own funds, which may not be obtained by pledging or early withdrawal of second-pillar pension assets, and compulsory amortisation of loans. A counter-cyclical buffer (CCB) was activated at the beginning of 2013 and obliges banks to hold additional common equity Tier 1 capital based on their risk-weighted mortgage positions secured by residential real estate in Switzerland. In January 2014, the CCB was increased from 1% to 2%. Despite these measures, house prices remain high and the risk to the banking sector elevated.

Introduction

Over the past decade real estate prices in Switzerland have been increasing much faster than household incomes, and rental vacancy rates have remained very low. The growth in the demand for housing has been robust, particularly driven by strong inflows of migrants and the low cost of borrowing. The results is that, while neither the quality nor the availability of housing pose serious problems in Switzerland, the Swiss spend a high proportion of their disposable incomes on housing. Indeed, housing is expensive in Switzerland, not just in absolute terms but also relative to the country's comparatively high level of per capita income (Figure 1.1). One of the reasons for this is the high cost of construction, as was discussed in the 2009 *Survey*, so that the supply response has been insufficient. This has been exacerbated by, among other things, the poor availability of land and strict construction codes.

Household debt levels are high, largely due to mortgage loans. The other side of the coin is that Swiss banks are highly exposed to the housing market, and in the event of a major downward adjustment in prices, mortgage lenders might find themselves in trouble, with potentially serious implications for the broader economy. Authorities in Switzerland have been taking measures to minimise and manage this risk, with some success. While continued short-term vigilance is surely required, there are also longer-term measures that could help avoid a recurrence of the significant housing cycles seen in Switzerland over the past 50 years.

Figure 1.1. **Affordability and absolute cost of housing in selected OECD countries, 2011**

Sample average = 100

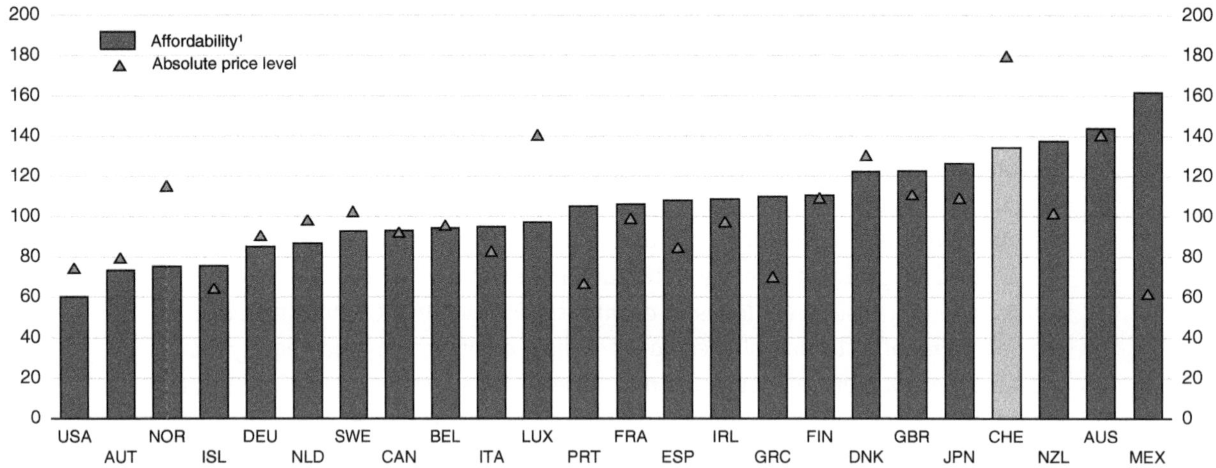

1. Calculated using PPP prices for housing-related expenditure (housing, water, electricity, gas and other fuels) divided by GNI per capita (PPP, constant 2011 international dollars).

Source: *OECD Purchasing Power Parities Database*; and *World Bank World Development Indicators Database*.

StatLink http://dx.doi.org/10.1787/888933292441

This chapter examines recent developments in the Swiss housing market. First, the factors driving housing-market developments are discussed, including those underlying both supply and demand. On the demand side, low interest rates and high population growth, smaller family units, driven in particular by strong immigration, are the most important. The reasons for low homeownership are also examined. Then supply-side aspects are discussed, including the importance of rigidities in making land available for residential development, particularly in high-demand areas, in explaining the supply-demand imbalance. The chapter concludes by making policy recommendations aimed to dampen the Swiss housing cycle.

Developments in the Swiss housing market

There have been three distinct cycles in the Swiss housing market since the beginning of the 1970s (Figure 1.2), which have generally followed the broader business cycle: one that peaked in 1973, a second that culminated in 1989, and a third is ongoing. The first two booms were of similar amplitude, as were their durations (defined as sustained CPI-adjusted appreciation of over 5% per annum), but the current one has less amplitude but a longer duration. In all three there have been heterogeneous regional developments. Most notably, in the current cycle, house price increases in Geneva have outpaced those elsewhere, while gains in the other major metropolitan areas have also been robust. Indeed, in the canton of Geneva itself, the price of apartments has more than tripled since 2000, while the average across all of Switzerland has been just over half that (Figure 1.3). In the north-western and some central cantons, price appreciation of houses rather than apartments has been considerably more modest, with price increases of around 50% since 2000.

Figure 1.2. **House prices in Switzerland over recent cycles**

Index, 14 quarters before the peak = 100[1]

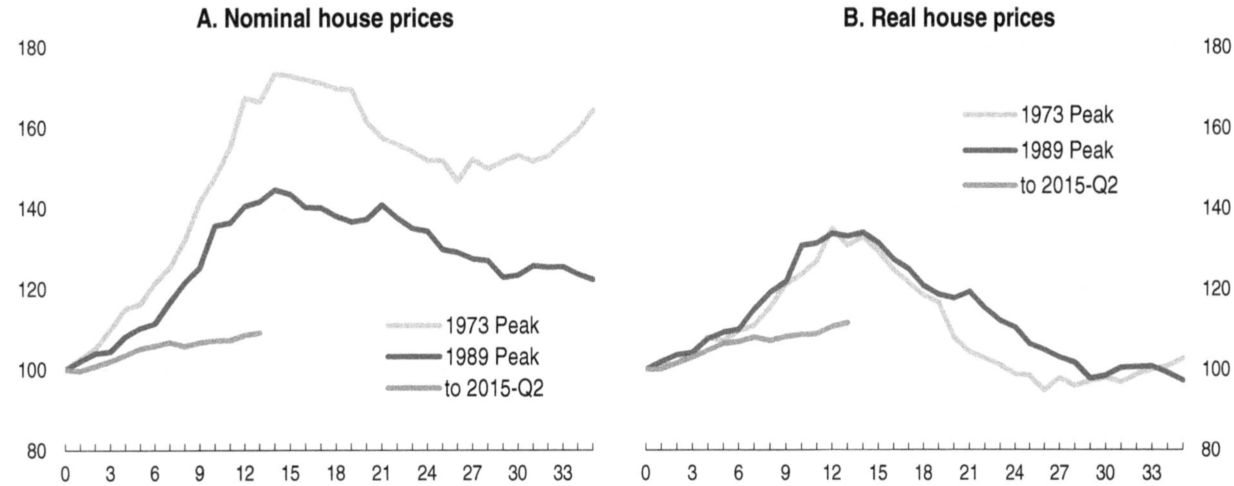

1. The series for the most recent cycle has yet to peak so the chart shows the latest 14 quarters.

Source: OECD House Price Database.

StatLink http://dx.doi.org/10.1787/888933292458

The real estate boom of the 1980s took place against the background of an economic boom in the second half of the decade and the introduction of the obligatory second pillar in the Swiss pension system. The economic boom drew large numbers of foreign workers, particularly from Yugoslavia, which significantly shifted demand in the housing market.

Figure 1.3. **Real estate prices by canton**

Apartments, increase in price indices, year 2000 = 100

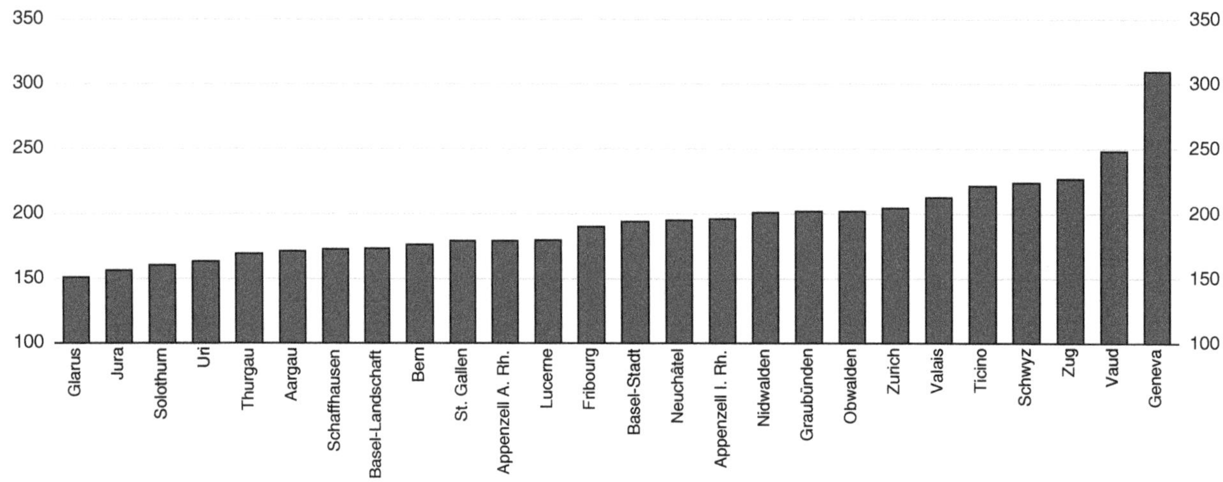

Source: Fahrländer Partner.

StatLink http://dx.doi.org/10.1787/888933292460

Moreover, rising incomes and relatively low interest rates improved the housing affordability. To cover the growing demand for housing, construction boomed, but despite this increased activity, housing was in undersupply, especially in the larger urban areas. Vacancy rates fell to close to zero, and rising market rents were the consequence. Expanding urban areas also bore witness to the housing shortage. As the second pillar of the pension system matured, capital became concentrated in this system and was seeking returns. In the aftermath of the losses in the 1987 stock-market crash, pension funds, as well as individual investors, diverted more and more capital into real estate projects, which seemed to be a good hedge against the increasing inflation rate. Prices for investment properties rose dramatically, boosted by short-term speculation.

Several factors helped to trigger the real estate crisis of the 1990s. First, around 1990 an abrupt and sharp recession combined with ongoing high inflation and interest rates led to a significant decrease in demand for all kinds of properties. Second, since most mortgages had a variable interest rate, the high inflation and nominal interest rates of 8.5% reduced demand. Third, by the end of the 1980s strong demand and increasing market rents led to a significant increase in development and construction activity. When the business cycle peaked abruptly in 1990-91, many projects were still in the pipeline and came to market only after demand had crashed, and therefore vacancy rates rose significantly, and prices and market rents decreased. Markets in the Lake Geneva region reached their peak in 1990, while in the German-speaking regions the turning point was in 1991-92 (Fahrländer Partner, 2008).

The 1990s real estate bust led to a crisis of the mortgage banks, especially the small regional banks. The losses from unpaid interest due to insolvency did not do too much harm. Much more important was negative equity on the mortgages due to decreasing market values – between 1991 and 1996 prices for apartments fell by around 35% and in both Bern and Geneva by around 20%. Firms owning rental properties (non-financial corporations such as real estate funds and real estate companies) were especially exposed. In the five years leading up to crisis, the stock of mortgages held by non-financial corporations grew at a compound annual rate of approximately 12%, while mortgages held by households grew by an average 10% over the same period. Over the 1991-96 period, the Swiss Federal Banking Commission (SFBC) estimated a total loss from defaults of CHF 42 billion (around 10% of GDP). To a smaller extent this was due to write-offs on interest and principal for privately owned properties, but most of the losses were due to defaults on mortgages for investment properties, especially in the commercial sector. Smaller regional banks were especially hard hit. An estimated 100 of the 200 regional banks did not survive the crisis or lost their independence (BIS, 2004). Box 1.3 below provides further details.

The first decade of the new millennium saw the housing market reignite. Above-average economic growth, low interest rates, further liberalisation of migration rules, as well as the ability to fund the purchase of housing out of pension deposits led to a boom – of course starting from a low level. Despite an increase in construction of condominiums and single-family houses, and the expansion of urban areas, robust demand led to rapid price increases, which have now been ongoing for about 15 years.

By 2005 prices in some regions had eclipsed the peaks of the late 1980s, and there was already some speculation that the real estate market in Switzerland was "overheating" (Neff and Rauh, 2005; NZZ, 2005; Fahrländer, 2007). Since 2008, the Swiss National Bank (SNB) and other market observers have repeatedly warned of overheating in real estate markets. Several regulations by the Swiss Financial Market Supervisory Authority (FINMA) and the Federal Council, "self" regulation by the mortgage industry, as well as macroeconomic developments, brought a halt in the increases in prices for housing in some regions and a significant slowdown in most others, suggesting a soft landing. However, there are early signs of a reacceleration in some markets and sectors. Due to the high real yields in the real estate sector compared to other asset classes, prices of investment properties might rise still further.

Nevertheless, by most measures, recent developments in this housing cycle have not been as extreme as in the 1980s boom, and rental vacancy rates through the current cycle have never reached the lows seen at the end of the 1980s cycle. In 1989 the national average vacancy rate was 0.4%, while over the past few years it has hovered near 1% (Figure 1.4), a value that has been estimated by some to be almost in equilibrium (Thalmann, 2012). In some cantons in 1989, the vacancy rate was effectively zero. Also, as will be stated below, growth in mortgage volumes relative to real disposable income per capita has been considerably lower through this current cycle. On the other hand, the price-to-income ratio, particularly for owner-occupied apartments, has risen to levels last seen in 1989, and population growth, driven by sustained large migrant inflows, has been stronger over this cycle. And of course, interest rates have been much lower.

The structure of the Swiss housing market

One-third of the Swiss population lives in the agglomerations of the five largest cities: Zurich (1.1 million), Geneva (0.5 million), Basel (0.5 million), Bern (0.3 million) and Lausanne (0.3 million). Another third lives in the remaining urban areas, and a final third in the countryside. Strong population growth and improved infrastructure have accelerated urban sprawl. Only 7% of the land is allotted to settlements and urban areas, with the rest devoted to forests, woods, farmland and alpine farmland (68%), lakes and watercourses (4%), and unproductive land (21%). With a population of approximately 8.3 million, density is around 200 inhabitants per square kilometre. Since much of the land cannot be or is not used for residential purposes, the effective population density is, however, substantially higher than the average figure (Bourassa et al., 2010).

Figure 1.4. **Vacancy rates across cantons**

Percentage of total housing stock

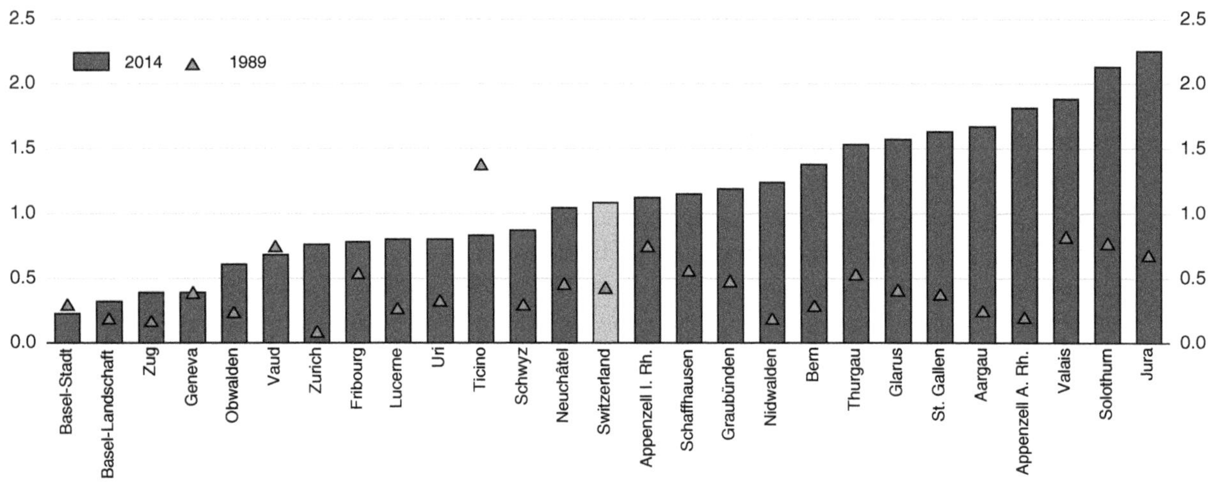

Source: Federal Office of Housing.

StatLink http://dx.doi.org/10.1787/888933292477

The level of homeownership is very low (see below), and about 60% of Swiss households rent an apartment or a single-family house (Figure 1.5) and a small but not insignificant number live in buildings with a co-operative ownership structure. These are typically in urban areas, with a particularly strong concentration in Zurich (see below). According to the latest available data, about 62% of rental apartments are owned by private investors, 28% by institutional investors such as pension funds, insurance companies, real estate funds and real estate companies, and about 10% by the public sector or non-profit co-operatives. Within the institutional investor category, pension funds constitute the largest owner class with almost 10% of the rental units in the country. Another striking figure is that close to 12% of housing units are second homes.

Figure 1.5. **Ownership structure across countries**

Per cent of dwelling stock, 2009

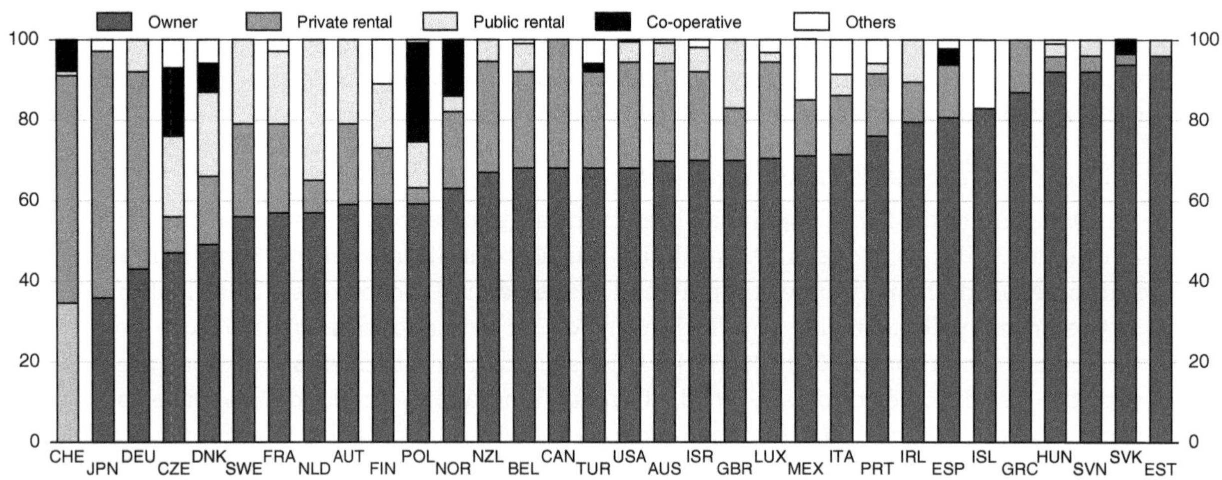

Source: Andrews D., et al. (2011), "Housing Markets and Structural Policies in OECD Countries", *OECD Economics Department Working Papers*, No. 836, OECD Publishing.

StatLink http://dx.doi.org/10.1787/888933292489

In 2013, about 66 700 arms-length real estate transactions worth an estimated CHF 56.8 billion were recorded (Fahrländer Partner, 2014). This transaction rate of approximately 3.4% of the stock is low, since homeowners tend to stay in their properties for a long time or, if moving, put them on the rental market (Andrews et al., 2011). More generally, residential mobility in Switzerland is around average, with about 16% of households changing residence over a two-year period: on a par with France but lower than in the Nordic countries.

Due to high prices and therefore relatively high rents, Swiss households spend around 23% of their gross income on housing, which is above the OECD average, on a par with Denmark and Luxembourg, and higher than France, Germany and Austria (Figure 1.6). According to the Eurostat SILC Survey, in 2013 around 38% of the Swiss population in the lowest income quintile lived in households where the total housing costs represented more than 40% of disposable income. This is higher than Belgium, France and Austria but lower than Germany and the Netherlands. Indeed, the housing cost "overburden rate" (the percentage of the population living in households where the total housing costs represent more than 40% of disposable income) for low-income earners in Switzerland is well above the average for European countries (OECD, 2011). High spending on housing is in part due to relatively expensive rents in Switzerland – second only to Japan, according to some studies (Andrews et al., 2011). The trend in many OECD countries has been for spending shares on housing to rise in recent years, with financial deregulation and lower interest rates making borrowing easier and cheaper and therefore boosting homeownership rates and thereby lifting spending on housing. Moreover, prices have also risen, as have rents, adding to upward pressure on spending on housing. That said, in Switzerland the increase in the share of spending on housing has been modest, probably due to rent controls and the still low levels of homeownership.

Figure 1.6. **Housing expenditures in OECD countries**

Percentage of household gross disposable income,[1] 2012 or latest available year

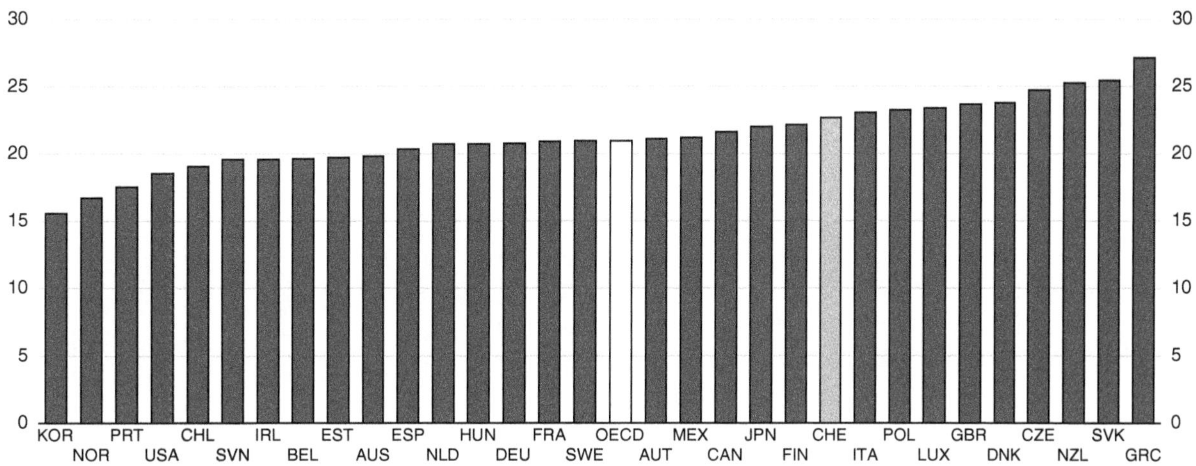

Note: Housing expenditures include actual and imputed rents, expenditure on maintenance and repair of the dwelling, on water supply, electricity, gas and other fuels, furniture, furnishings and household equipment, goods and services for routine maintenance of the house. Data refer to 2012 with the exception of 2011 for Japan, New Zealand and Switzerland and 2010 for Canada.

1. Gross of depreciation but after taxes and transfers as well as social transfers in kind such as education and health care.

Source: OECD calculations based on OECD Better Life Index (2014); and *OECD National Accounts Statistics Database*.

StatLink http://dx.doi.org/10.1787/888933292495

Home ownership rates are low but increasing

Private home ownership rates in Switzerland are low, at around 44% (2013; population living in private home ownership), which is the lowest in Europe and likely in the OECD by a significant margin (Figure 1.7). Promoting the private ownership of homes is enshrined in the Federal Constitution (Section 8, Article 108). The principle vehicle for this, introduced in 1995, is letting residents draw on their second- and third-pillar pension assets to fund part of the down payment to buy a home. The pension system can also be used to fund refurbishments. Research suggests a number of factors explain the low rates of private home ownership. Bourassa and Hoesli (2006) find that high house prices – relative to rents and to household incomes and wealth – are the most important cause. Within Switzerland, home ownership rates vary considerably from one area to another. The degree of urbanisation is an important determinant of this variation, with Geneva and Basel (14% and 17%, respectively) having the lowest rates in the country, and the Jura and Valais the highest (58% and 56%, respectively). However, in this case urbanisation may be a proxy for relative affordability. Another unique feature of Swiss home ownership is that the average age at which people become home owners is between 35 and 40 years; this is relatively late by international comparison and is consistent with the affordability hypothesis. Andrews and Caldera Sánchez (2011) find that, while age structure and other non-age factors account for some of the change in home ownership in Switzerland in the period 1995-2005, a large part remains unexplained.

In many countries home ownership is commonly a form of saving for retirement, in addition to pension savings and life insurance. However, in Switzerland, present arrangements for the taxation of savings held in pension funds and life insurance companies are very favourable, possibly also explaining low home ownership rates. Contributions to earnings-related pension schemes have been compulsory only since 1985, and the Swiss have accumulated substantial pension fund assets (113% of GDP in 2013) by international comparison. Life insurance company assets (51% of GDP in 2013) are also

Figure 1.7. **Home ownership in selected European countries, 2014**[1]

Percentage of all persons living in private households

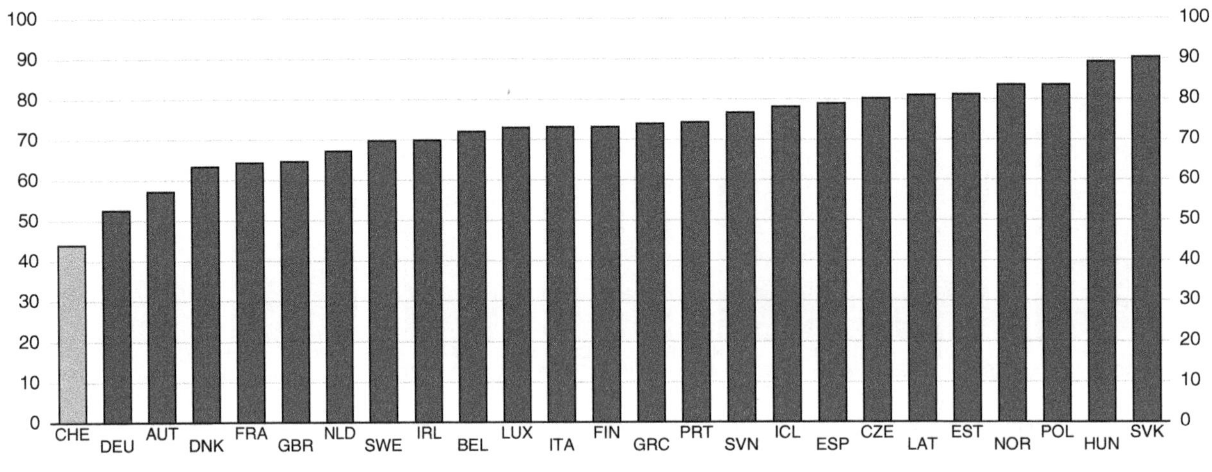

1. Or latest year available (2013 for Switzerland).

Source: Eurostat, Statistics on Income and Living Conditions (distribution of population by tenure status).

StatLink http://dx.doi.org/10.1787/888933292505

high. Indeed, the combined total of pension fund and life insurance assets (164% of GDP) is among the highest in the OECD (Figure 1.8). These figures suggest that these incentives contribute to the accumulation of this form of long-term savings, at the expense of home ownership (Carey et al., 1999).

Figure 1.8. **Pension and life insurance assets in OECD countries, 2013**

As a percentage of GDP

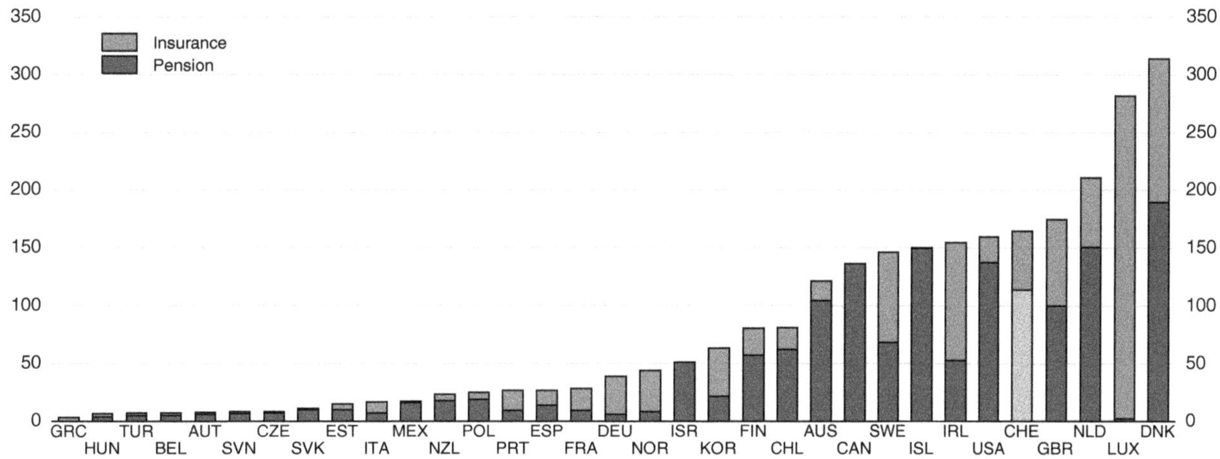

Source: OECD Insurance Statistics; OECD Pension Statistics; and *OECD Annual National Accounts Database.*

StatLink http://dx.doi.org/10.1787/888933292512

Drivers of developments in the housing market

It is difficult to determine if the price increases seen in the Swiss housing market over the past 15 years are sustainable: the indicators are mixed. Nevertheless, policy responses depend to a large extent on such a judgement. A number of factors suggest that part of the price appreciation has been driven by a number of factors, including a strong economy, population increases (including higher immigration), demand from investors, increased affordability in the short term due to lower interest rates and easier availability of mortgage financing. These may have resulted in high demand and low rental vacancies. At the same time, a number of constraints impede supply responsiveness, including the lack of available land due to zoning regulations, strict construction standards, lock-in effects from capital gains taxation, and low nominal rental yields due to high prices and rent controls.

Aside from fundamental demand and supply determinants, low returns in other investment assets may also be driving "search-for-yield" behaviour, especially by institutional investors (pension funds). The net impact of all these factors is difficult to judge, but it is a critical assessment from the standpoint of macro-prudential policy formulation – both in terms of protecting a potentially over-exposed banking sector, as well as possibly over-leveraged households – given the impact that bursting a bubble would have on the economy and social welfare more generally.

Mortgage interest rates and affordability

Interest rates directly influence the market for owner-occupied property, as well as the market for investment property, through the affordability of lending. Moreover, low mortgage interest rates sustained for an extended period are a feature associated with real estate bubbles in many countries (Hott and Jokipii, 2012). As in almost all OECD countries, Swiss mortgage interest rates have been falling since mid-2008 and are currently at unprecedentedly low levels (Figure 1.9). The average interest rate on new mortgages in 1993 was 6.2%, in 2003 3.4% and in 2013 less than 2%. Moreover, it is also the case that Swiss interest rates have been consistently below those in almost all other OECD countries (with the notable exception of Japan) for many years. In recent years, interest rates have been especially low, as the central bank has been trying to prevent the appreciation of the Swiss franc.

Figure 1.9. **Mortgage interest rates in Switzerland**

Percentage points

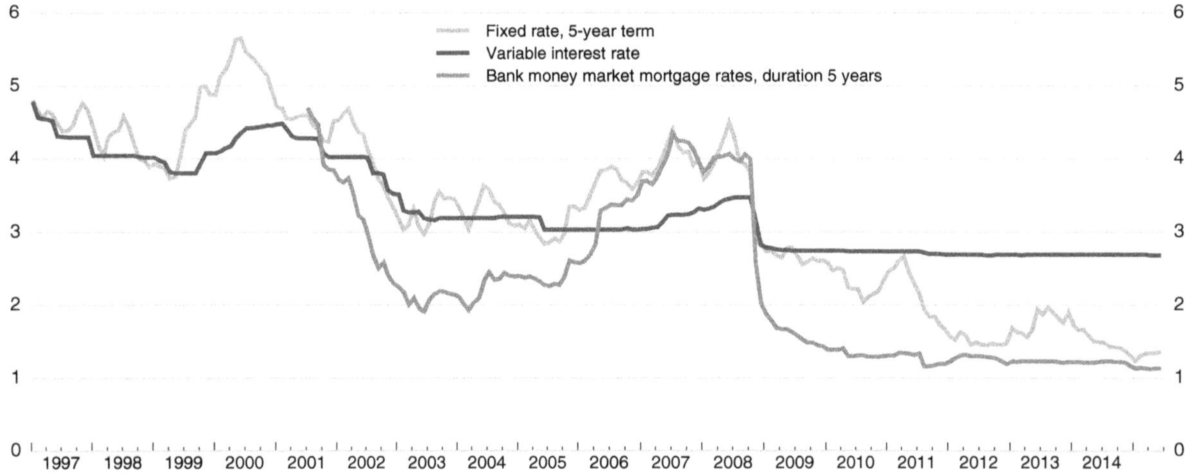

Source: Swiss National Bank.

StatLink http://dx.doi.org/10.1787/888933292529

A crude metric of housing affordability is the price-to-income ratio, which simply measures the average quality-adjusted price of housing against disposable income. It does not consider population growth as well as the actual cost of borrowing, taxation and upkeep. According to this measure, housing affordability is fairly high by historical standards, despite a steady increase in the price-to-income ratio since the beginning of the 2000s (Figure 1.10, Panel A). Moreover, in contrast with most other OECD countries, the Swiss price-to-income ratio has remained relatively low and stable compared to the mid-1980s (Panel B). However, affordability is below its historical average if population growth is taken into account.

A better measure of housing affordability would take into account changes in the cost of borrowing and property maintenance, in addition to the cost of housing itself. Credit Suisse's Housing Affordability Index (HAI), calculated for condominiums and single-family homes, shows the general burden of housing costs on home owners' budgets (Figure 1.11, Panel A). Due to low mortgage rates and the steady growth in household incomes, housing costs have shrunk as a share of household budgets in the recent past, even though they remain high by OECD standards. Analysis based on census and micro-census data show that, in recent years especially, Swiss lower- and middle-class households in particular increased their home ownership rates (Fahrländer Partner and sotomo, 2014). This development has also been driven by the possibility to tap into compulsory pension savings to help finance the necessary 20% down payment for a mortgage-financed purchase.

Figure 1.10. **Housing price-to-income ratios**

Index, 1985 = 100

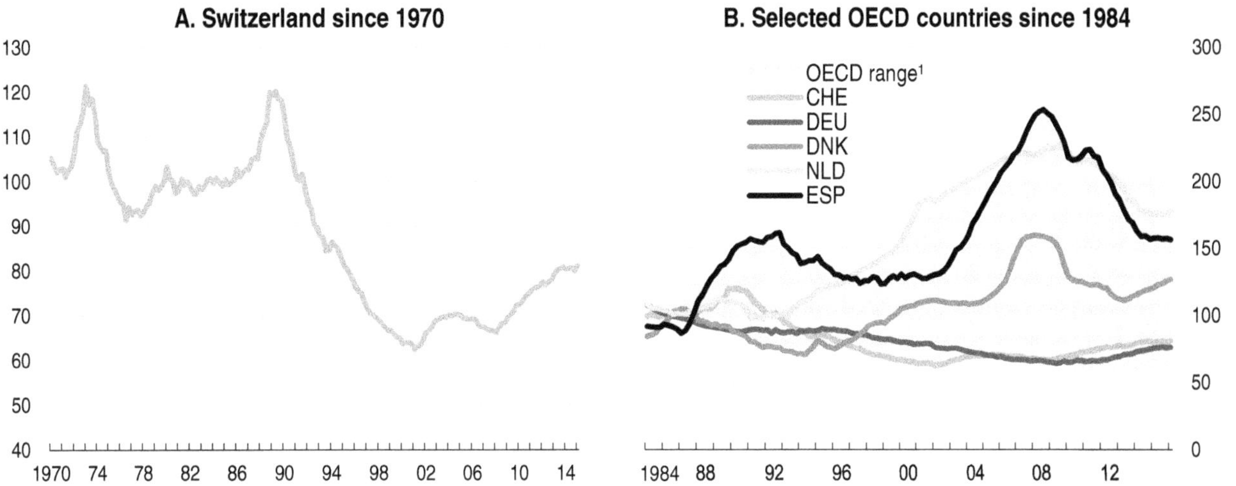

1. All OECD countries except for Chile, Iceland, Israel, Mexico, Poland and Turkey for which no data are available.

Source: OECD House Price Database.

StatLink http://dx.doi.org/10.1787/888933292530

Figure 1.11. **Housing affordability and costs**

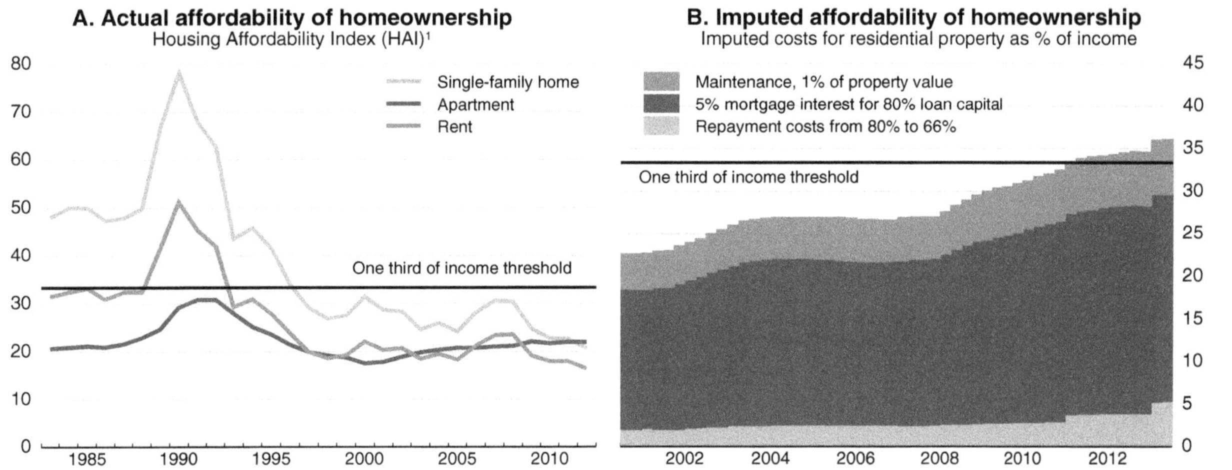

1. Credit Suisse's Housing Affordability Index (HAI) shows the general burden of housing costs on homeowners' budget by type of housing.

Source: Credit Suisse.

StatLink http://dx.doi.org/10.1787/888933292545

In assessing the eligibility for mortgages, Swiss banks use a "golden rule", which stipulates that mortgage and running costs should not exceed one third of the household's income. In calculating this ratio for the purposes of assessing eligibility to borrow, rather than the current mortgage interest rate it is current practice for Swiss banks to apply an interest rate of 5% with an additional 1% for amortisation and 1% of the property value for maintenance. In the present circumstances, this constitutes a significant safety margin, and, with the steady decline in market interest rates since the global financial crisis, a significant wedge has opened up between affordability calculated using the market interest rate and the assumed 5% rate. As Credit Suisse shows, affordability with imputed long-term averages (80% loan-to-value, 5-year fixed mortgage) has fallen significantly since the year 2000 (Figure 1.11, Panel B), and currently, for the average household, the estimated cost of home ownership exceeds the one-third golden rule (Credit Suisse, 2015). This shows that for a significant share of Swiss households home ownership remains unaffordable.

Mortgage availability

In addition to the reduced cost of borrowing from lower interest rates, the increased availability of mortgages and easier options for funding down payments are also likely to have fuelled demand for real estate. Except for a two-year spell between 2006 and 2008, mortgage lending growth has significantly exceeded increases in household disposable income over the past decade and a half (Figure 1.12).

One significant change that has facilitated greater housing market activity is the ability to access pension funds for down payments for residential property purchase. Under certain conditions, it is possible to retrieve or to pledge pension savings to buy housing. This has been the case since 1990 for third-pillar pensions and since 1995 for second-pillar pensions and is part of the political promotion of home ownership stipulated in article 108 of the Federal Constitution. According to UBS, every year 35 000 to 40 000 people use second-pillar funds to buy housing or to fund refurbishments (UBS, 2014). UBS estimates that at least 10% of today's transactions involving single-family properties are at least partly funded out of the second pillar. However, due to rising real estate risks, in 2012 the authorities approved a banking-sector "self" regulation to impose a minimum down payment of 10% of the lending value of the property from the borrower's own funds, which may not be obtained by pledging or early withdrawal of second-pillar pension assets. This minimum cash down payment requirement indirectly reduces the use of second-pillar pension assets. Moreover, there has recently been political discussion about abolishing recourse to the second pillar, first for some groups of savers but ultimately with the aim of removing this right for all. This is a measure that authorities should keep in their back pocket as a last resort.

Figure 1.12. **Mortgage volumes and household disposable income**

Year-on-year % change

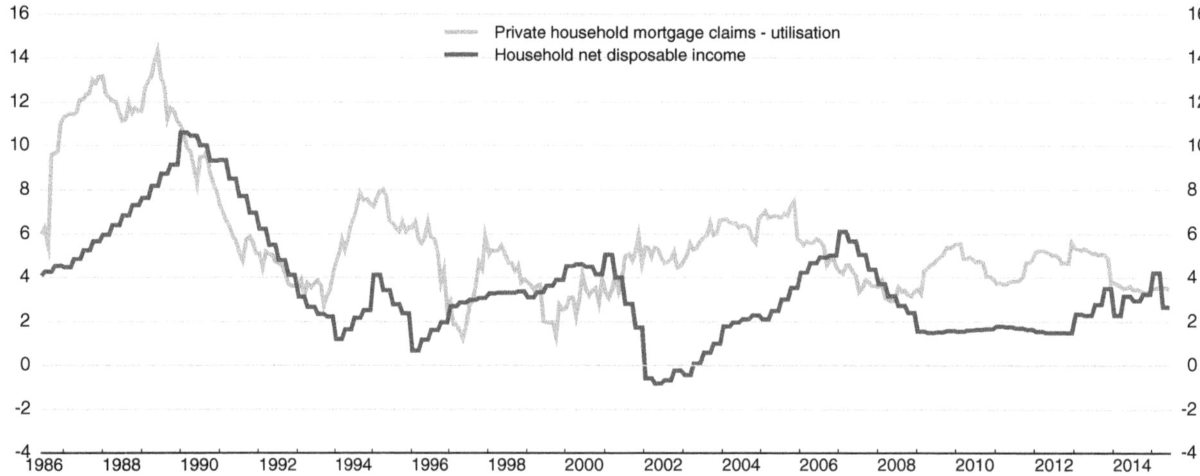

Source: Swiss National Bank; *OECD Economic Outlook 97 Database* (and updates); and OECD calculations.

StatLink http://dx.doi.org/10.1787/888933292557

Demographics

The permanent resident population of Switzerland has grown by 13% since 2000, or around 900 000 people (Figure 1.13). The annual population increase of over 1% over the past several years is among the highest in the OECD. Of this, migration accounted for around 700 000 people or nearly 80% of the increase. Migration-driven population growth has been particularly strong since the Agreement on the Free Movement of Persons with the European Union came into force on 1 June 2002. The resulting rapid rise in household formation has, without a doubt, fuelled the demand for housing in Switzerland over the past decade and a half.

Figure 1.13. **Migration and natural population growth**

Per cent growth

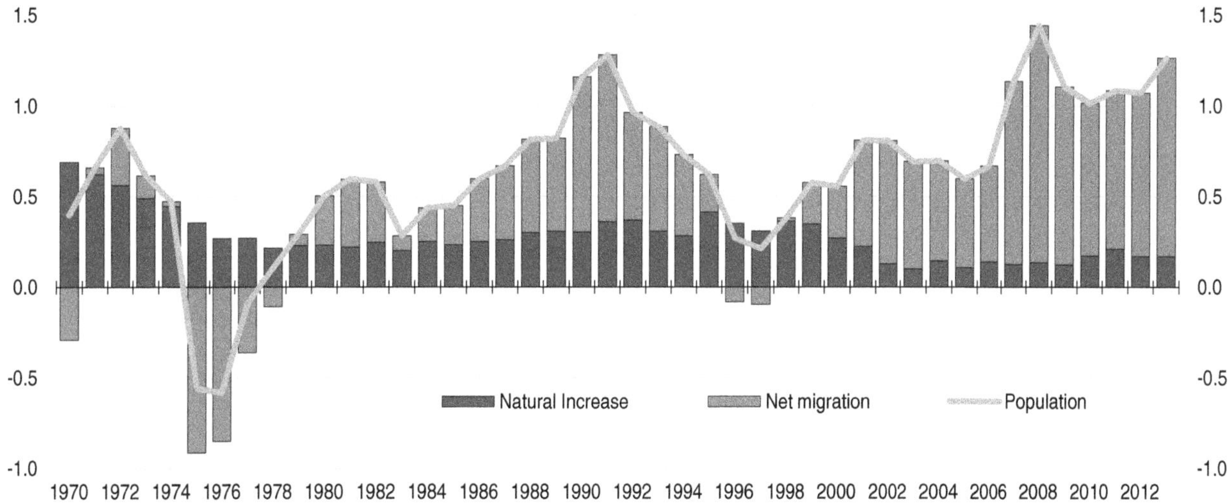

Source: OECD Population and Vital Statistics Database.

StatLink http://dx.doi.org/10.1787/888933292563

Whereas in the 1980s and 1990s the Swiss quota system was designed for low skilled seasonal workers, the more recent migration policy featuring freedom of movement with the EU/EFTA countries, as well as quotas for high skilled immigrants and additional allotments for expatriates, is much more responsive to the needs of the economy. Due to great success in the attraction of companies from abroad, comparatively high incomes and quality of life in general, more high skilled immigrants have settled in Switzerland. Overall, the skill structure of recent immigrants is more or less comparable to that of the local population, since high-income immigration is usually accompanied by low-skill immigration to provide all the necessary additional services (Zürcher Kantonalbank, 2010). Indeed, Switzerland is one of the few OECD countries that draws a balanced mix of both higher and lower skilled migrants (OECD, 2013), although in recent years migration has become more qualified, mainly driven by free mobility with the EU/EFTA (Liebig et al., 2012). Moreover, the trend towards smaller family units has been a factor in increasing the demand for housing in Switzerland. Indeed, the average size of migrant households coming to Switzerland is only marginally larger than Swiss-born households (OECD, 2015), which reinforces the already small household size, which, at 2.2 persons, is among the smallest in Europe and well below the OECD average of 2.7, down from 3.4 in 1960.

Against the background of high unemployment in some of the surrounding countries and comparatively strong economic growth in Switzerland (see below), net immigration is expected to stay high in the coming years, although the acceptance of the initiative against mass immigration in February 2014 may have a disruptive effect starting in 2017 when it must be implemented and perhaps even earlier due to the uncertainty effects (Box 1.1).

Box 1.1. **Changes in Swiss migration policy**

On 9 February 2014 some 50.3% of the Swiss population accepted an initiative against "mass immigration", but the people clearly refused an initiative for much more restrictive regulation of immigration in November of the same year. The Swiss parliament has until February 2017 to design the new immigration rules, and the government will have to set quotas for all kinds and origins of immigrants, including cross-border commuters. Since quotas already exist for non-European immigration, the new regulation will especially apply to immigrants from the EU/EFTA. This policy change might not be possible without a revision of the accord of free movement of persons with the European Union. In February 2015 the Swiss Federal Council drafted the necessary changes to the relevant law and articulated a mandate to negotiate with the EU. According to this draft, quotas should be set annually for new immigration but not for changes in immigration status. The draft law requires that quotas be set in consultation with cantons and a new immigration commission.

Household income growth

Switzerland has enjoyed strong economic growth over the past decade coinciding with a booming housing market. In the decade to 2013, Switzerland had the seventh highest rate of real GDP growth in the OECD. This has underpinned a strongly performing labour market and rising household incomes. However, in terms of real per capita disposable income growth, Switzerland's ranking drops to 13th. As illustrated in the previous *Survey*, rapid population increases over this period have led to robust overall GDP growth, but productivity gains have been weaker.

Search for yield

Yields on Swiss government bonds have fallen dramatically, which has put institutional investors in a tight spot. For instance, as pension funds have to guarantee a certain minimum return (currently 1.75%) to mandatory second-pillar pension savings, they have a problem since the yield on the "risk free" asset, a 10-year Swiss Confederation bond, currently stands at 0.1%. At the same time, the pension system alone faces an influx of CHF 50 billion in new savings per year that needs to be invested (BSV, 2014). Like many other institutional investors, the pension funds have turned to real estate as an asset class where acceptable yields can be realised. The current gross return on buy-to-let properties is around 3 to 4%, which remains attractive compared to other asset classes (globalpropertyguide.com). Consequently, demand for investment property, especially apartment buildings, has been rising sharply in recent years, not only by institutional but also by individual investors, and as demand has boosted prices, nominal gross yields have dropped to levels never seen before. Banks, insurance companies and pension funds face a portfolio dilemma: either they invest their funds in real estate, thereby diminishing returns on their existing real estate portfolios, or they turn to the stock market with its higher short-term volatility.

Demand from non-residents

With the onset of the global financial crisis in 2008, and again with the euro area crisis starting in 2011, Switzerland has been increasingly seen as a financial safe haven. However, there is little evidence of a surge in foreign money flowing into its residential housing market through that period. Moreover, restrictions on non-residents' residential real estate purchases, including for buy-to-let, have long been in place, curtailing safe-haven investments in this sector (Box 1.2). That said, immigrants from EU/EFTA and other immigrants with permanent residency are not considered as "persons abroad" for the purposes of these restrictions, and, as noted above, their numbers have increased considerably since 2002.

Box 1.2. **Regulations for foreigners on the Swiss housing market ("Lex Koller")**

The regulation of investment in real estate by "persons abroad" has a long history in Switzerland, going back to the 1950s. The purchase of commercial properties was liberalised in 1997, but residential purchases continue to be regulated by the so-called "Lex Koller" rules. According to these regulations, "persons abroad" are restricted to buying residences in certain areas of the country – mainly in the touristic areas in the Alps, and only up to a certain annual quota. Moreover, the size of properties is typically restricted to a "net" living area of no more than 200 m^2 and the total property being no more than 1000 m2. Real estate (such as dwellings, private houses, city apartments, tenements, etc.) in "non-tourist" locations is subject to a very stringent approval process, and in practice this approval is seldom granted to non-residents. Additionally, a maximum of one third of the gross area in each property may be sold to foreigners, and there is a minimum market value of around CHF 700 000. That said, rules vary from canton to canton and even across municipalities within cantons. However, immigrants from EU/EFTA and other immigrants with permanent residency are not considered as "persons abroad" for the purposes of this regulation, and their numbers have increased considerably since 2002. The possibility for non-residents to invest in Swiss housing through shares in listed companies has existed since 2005. Today some foreign-controlled construction companies are considered as "persons abroad" and have problems investing in land for development if more than 10% of the buildable floor space is suitable for housing.

In 2005 the Swiss government started a process to abolish the "Lex Koller" rules, but after the onset of the global financial crisis the parliament refused the abolition (last ballots were cast in parliament on 26 November 2014). Attempts to re-regulate the commercial property sector are also now being discussed. In 2012, the Swiss people voted for the establishment of a new article in the constitution that would limit the quota of second homes at the communal level to 20% of the housing stock. The corresponding new law has been approved by the Parliament but has not yet entered into force. In the future, it will affect and further restrict the purchase of second homes also by foreigners, since the share of second homes in many touristic regions is already at 20% or above.

Supply

In Switzerland, as in other OECD countries, residential investment has typically responded to changes in population growth, whether from natural increases or net migration. However, it has failed to respond to the surge in population growth as it once would have, with the housing investment-to-GDP ratio remaining at very low levels since the beginning of the 2000s (Figure 1.14). The same pattern is evident in a number of other OECD countries including Australia, Denmark, Finland, Norway and Sweden. Housing investment's share in nominal GDP has remained steady at around 4% of GDP and was among the lowest in the OECD until 2009 when the housing cycle crashed in many OECD countries.

This low level of household investment was despite the fact that population growth has been among the fastest in the OECD and that Swiss construction costs are among the highest in absolute terms and relative to both the average price of goods and the price of other fixed investment spending (OECD PPP database). This may help to explain the rapid increases in house prices since the early 2000s. Caldera Sánchez and Johansson (2013) find that the supply response to prices changes in Switzerland is the lowest in their sample of 21 OECD countries (Figure 1.15, Panel A) and suggest that one reason for this might be the stringency of the relevant regulation, including the time taken to obtain building permits (Panel B). Using a stock-flow model of the Swiss housing market, Steiner (2010) finds that supply-demand disequilibria can endure for extended periods of time during which prices can overshoot. She attributes these slow dynamics in part to the slow planning process for residential construction in Switzerland.

Figure 1.14. **Housing investment in selected countries**

Percentage of GDP

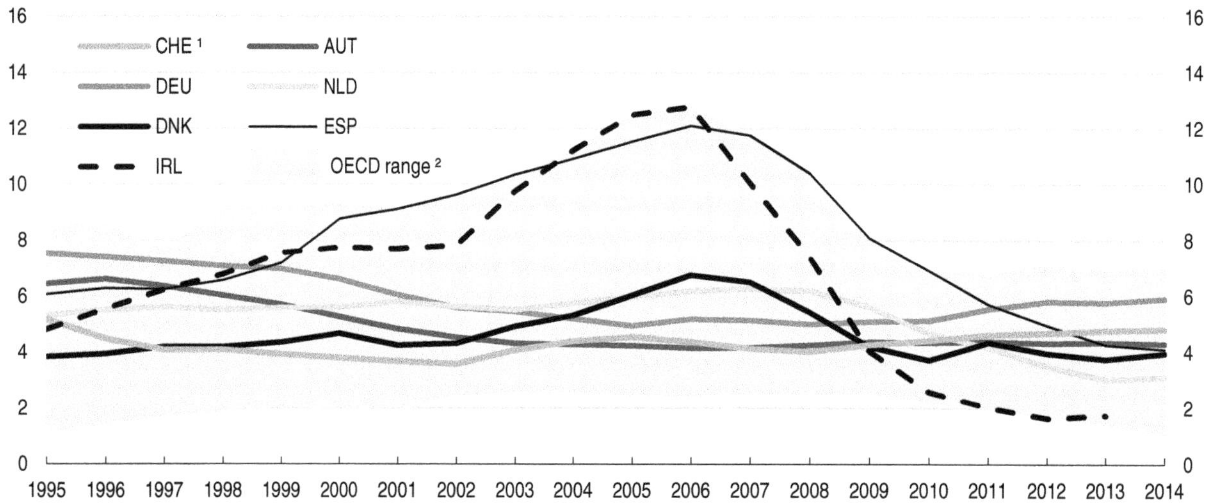

1. For Switzerland data refer to total investment in dwellings, excluding land.
2. Excluding countries where data is not available for the full period (Mexico and Turkey).

Source: *OECD Economic Outlook 97 Database* (and updates); and OECD staff estimates.

StatLink http://dx.doi.org/10.1787/888933292579

Spatial planning

Given Switzerland's high population density and relatively rapid demographic growth, some of the main aims of its spatial planning regulations have been to preserve agricultural lands and natural landscapes by containing urban sprawl and promoting the densification of already urbanised areas. Nevertheless, there is no shortage of building land to meet the demand for residential housing (Fahrländer Partner, 2008). However, the existing building zones are spatially not optimally distributed: those regions with lower demand tend to have the largest reserves, while in many urban areas building land for residential use is scarce. Furthermore, urban planning laws give neighbours of potential

Figure 1.15. **Housing supply responsiveness in selected countries**

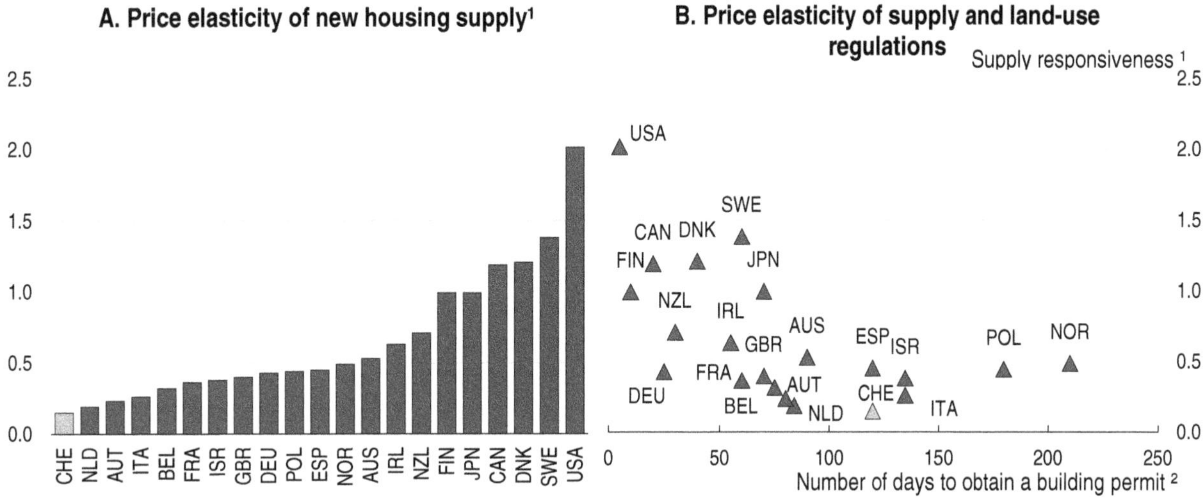

1. Estimates of the long-run price elasticity of new housing supply where new supply is measured by residential investment (see Caldera Sánchez and Johansson (2011)).
2. The number of days to obtain a building permit is obtained from the World Bank Doing Business (2009) indicators.

Source: Caldera Sánchez, A. and Å. Johansson (2013), "The price responsiveness of housing supply in OECD countries", *Journal of Housing Economics*, Volume 22, Issue 3, September, pp. 231-49.

StatLink http://dx.doi.org/10.1787/888933292580

construction sites a lot of leverage to delay the planning and construction process, which mainly affects large housing schemes in densely populated areas. Due to the lack of viable projects, developers have been pushed into ever more peripheral areas, thus further exacerbating urban sprawl. The Federal Law on Spatial Planning strongly influences the extent and characteristics of building zones and therefore largely defines the supply side of the housing market in metropolitan areas. That said, international evidence shows that where local governments receive a large share of taxes paid by their residents, such as in Switzerland, Germany and the United States, authorities tend to adopt a positive attitude towards development and compete to attract households (Evans and Hartwich, 2005).

The Federal Law lays down the principles of Swiss spatial planning, although the implementing legislation is cantonal, and zoning and land planning is done at the municipal level. Most cantons have joined a concordat harmonising some construction regulations. Furthermore, the Federal Law has recently been revised to deal with urban sprawl, namely through measures for removing excessively large development areas, which tend to remain unutilised for longer periods, and stimulating higher-density urban development (ARE, 2014a). For this purpose, the cantons must implement new tools to manage their settlement areas. In December 2014 the Federal Council proposed another set of revisions to address the protection of agricultural land, the co-ordination of transport and energy infrastructures with spatial development, as well as cross-border spatial-planning initiatives (ARE, 2014b). Both revisions are consistent with the trend to shifting planning competences from the municipal to the cantonal authorities. The revised law provides more detail and precision as regards cantonal tasks in spatial planning.

The main instrument for land planning is a legally binding municipal-level land-use plan, which is updated every 15 years. Zoning an area for settlement creates a duty for the municipality to build infrastructure, and in case of rezoning to no longer be residential, to compensate landowners. Additionally, it is not possible for municipalities to buy the land before zoning it for settlement purposes, as buying and selling agricultural land is permitted only for farmers (with only a few possible exceptions). Some municipalities also prepare Municipal Structure Plans, which encompass their entire territory and aim to set the main framework for future urban development.

The revised Federal Law strongly promotes densification, especially in areas with above-average accessibility by public transport. Several cities have taken measures to increase allowed density, notably the cities of Geneva and Zurich. Furthermore, instruments for private investors and public authorities to co-operate in the mobilisation of potential increases in the density of existing zones and structures (inner development) reserves have also been introduced in the last few years. For instance, in February 2015 the government of the Canton of Zurich published plans to increase density by 20% and more in certain areas surrounding the city of Zurich itself. The supply of land for residential construction in high-demand areas could be increased by taxing land that has been rezoned for real estate but has remained undeveloped for more than, say, five years.

But in the end it is the owner of the property who decides if and when s/he wants to realise this potential. When a building nears the end of its lifetime, densification usually takes place, because from the owner's point of view it makes economic sense to construct as much floor space as possible. In cases where a building is still in good shape, it is much harder to achieve a higher density, either because the owner does not want to demolish and reconstruct, or because the building's structural conditions prevent the addition of an additional storey. Furthermore, the owner often is unaware that there exists a potential for higher density on the property. The capacity for inner development should be reassessed, and a programme of audits of individual properties that feature potential for added-value densification should be instituted, and this information should be provided to property owners.

Switzerland's 26 cantons each have different building laws and codes. The barriers this presents to cheaper housing construction were discussed in the 2009 *Survey*. Heterogeneous construction codes and standards reduce the potential for competition as compliance costs for construction firms operating across jurisdictions are higher. Differentiated labour laws across cantons also inhibit competition in the construction industry by preventing companies from exploiting economies of scale (OECD, 2009).

Environmental standards

In general, economic costs of environmental regulations are relatively low in Switzerland, reflecting comparatively low administrative burdens associated with permitting and licencing (Koźluk, 2014). However, the environmental impact of the housing sector is not inconsiderable. Given that more than a third of Swiss energy consumption is used to heat buildings and water, the energy-saving potential of this sector is huge. Switzerland has adopted the MINERGIE standard for new and refurbished low-energy-consumption buildings. This standard is mutually supported by the Confederation and the cantons. Building a property according to MINERGIE standards is about 10% more expensive, but compared to a conventional building a MINERGIE-certified structure has up to 60% lower energy costs. As of April 2015, there were around 15 000 individual residences and 9 300 apartments with MINERGIE certification, including both newly constructed and renovated dwellings (www.minergie.ch/liste-des-batiments.html).

Most cantons offer financial incentives in the form of subsidies and grants for new or renovated MINERGIE buildings. A major vehicle for this is the federally sponsored Building Renovation Programme, launched in 2010 and taking over where the Climate Cent Buildings Programme left off. The Programme has been allocated CHF 300 million annually for 10 years and will both fund improved insulation in homes built before 2000, as well as subsidise energy-efficient construction. However, Salvi and Syz (2011) find that in Switzerland, after taking into account other factors, subsidies do not seem to trigger additional green housing activity. The authors conjecture that, as the median subsidy payment accounts for just about a tenth of the extra building cost associated with the MINERGIE certification, the subsidies are too small to encourage much new certified construction.

While in general value-preserving expenditures (maintenance and upkeep) on rental properties can be deducted from a landlord's taxable income, value-adding expenditures that entitle the landlord to raise the rent are not deductible. The exception is, however, for value-adding energy-efficiency renovations, which are both deductible and entitle the landlord to raise the rent. The landlord is allowed to pass 50-70% of the costs of renovation work onto the tenant. For tenants this can be unprofitable, because, although there are likely to be savings by virtue of lower heating and hot water costs, in practice the rent increases frequently exceed these savings (Wehrmüller, 2014).

Taxation of housing

The taxation of housing is an important policy instrument. In Switzerland home owners are subject to a wealth tax on their housing assets and also to the taxation of imputed rental income, against which mortgage interest and other expenses are deductible. At the cantonal and municipal levels a capital gains tax is imposed on the sale of both private and business property with usually progressive rates and lower taxes the longer the property is owned. Under certain circumstances, in most cantons capital gains made on the sale of real estate are also subject to a special surcharge if the duration of ownership is especially short.

Taxation of owner-occupied housing services, real estate wealth and property transactions

Switzerland is one of the few OECD countries where the imputed rent of private households living in their own home is taxed. Maintenance and insurance costs and mortgage interest payments are deductible, and if the owner does not utilise all the rooms, a further reduction in the imputed rental value is allowed in some cantons. In accordance with a verdict of the Federal Court, the imputed rental value on the cantonal level must not be lower than 60% of the market rent. Not surprisingly, this has resulted in estimated undervaluation of imputed rent of 30-40% across the most populous cantons (Bourassa and Hoesli, 2010). Moreover, property valuations used to calculate imputed rent are typically updated only infrequently, resulting in a weak link between taxes and house prices. Indeed, property taxes more generally have been found to reduce house price volatility, although the effect is small (Blöchliger et al., 2015).

Besides the taxation of imputed rents, properties are also subject to a wealth tax. Cantons levy annual wealth taxes, and the rates vary across cantons. Individuals pay taxes on privately owned business assets and real estate situated in Switzerland. The assets are supposed to be valued at market prices, yet many cantons use an official valuation that is generally less than market value and again updated only infrequently. Personal debts, mortgages, bank loans and overdrafts are deductible, as well as certain personal deductions and allowances depending on the canton. The wealth tax rate varies between cantons and municipalities, ranging from 0.1% to 0.96% for net taxable assets of 10 million Swiss francs (married couple without children). About half the cantons also levy an annual immovable property or land-based tax. The rates generally range from 0.02% to 0.3%. Here debts are not deductible.

A real estate transfer tax and tax on the realised capital gain applies to the sale of property. At cantonal and communal levels, capital gains on private immovable property are subject to special capital gains taxes (CGTs). However, subject to various conditions, that tax is deferred if the proceeds of the disposal are reinvested in other property used as a main residence in Switzerland. In general, a deduction is available based on the period of ownership, meaning that for a long-term ownership the tax is typically relatively low. In Geneva, for instance, the rate is 50% if the property is sold within two years of purchase, but 0% if the property is held for more than 25 years. Where ownership has been only for a short period, there is usually an additional speculation surcharge. The definitions of short-term and long-term ownership vary by canton. At the federal level, capital gains realised on real estate and other private assets are exempt from income taxation, unless the individual is deemed to have held the real estate as a business asset (e.g. when qualifying as a professional real estate broker or if investing in a construction consortium). Capital gains realised on business assets are included in profits and are subject to the general profits tax system, which is income tax for individuals or taxes on profits for legal entities. As a result, federal tax is levied in the general way, instead of separately as CGT.

Most cantons levy a real estate transfer tax on the transfer of ownership in a property based on the purchase price. If that price cannot be determined or appears arbitrary or unusually low, the market value is decisive. The rate varies by canton ranging between 0.5 and 3.5%. This tax is generally paid by the purchaser, but in some cantons it is split with the seller.

Lock-in effects from capital gains taxation

In so far as the real estate sector is concerned, the most important drawback of a tax on realised capital gains is its "lock-in" effect. Due to lock-in effects for existing homeowners, taxing (short-term) capital gains may be counterproductive to the objective of more stable housing prices, especially because it curbs the optimal reallocation of real estate properties based on the changing preferences of owners and potential buyers. Furthermore, Kugler and Lenz (2001) analyse the comparative performance of Swiss cantons by comparing trend economic growth rates in cantons with CGT against those without it. They found that the latter enjoyed an average short-(long-)run 2.2(3.1)% income gain relative to the former. Moreover, reducing the CGT rate has distributional effects: higher-income households are considerably more likely to own assets that can generate taxable gains than poorer households. Additionally, affluent households own most assets, realise most capital gains and in Switzerland pay most of their CGT at preferential rates. A CGT reduction would mainly benefit high-income taxpayers who are likely to save most of any tax break. Aregger et al. (2013) conclude that taxes on transaction values and capital gains in the real estate market are not suitable instruments of macro-prudential policy. Finally, reducing CGT rates may increase tax revenues by dramatically increasing realisations. While the effects of CGT rate changes continue to be debated and researched, the bulk of the international evidence suggests that reducing the CGT rate lowers revenues, even in the short run.

Reform of the taxation of owner-occupied housing

The objective of tax neutrality implies the equal treatment of consumption of housing services and of other goods, and of income from property and income from other assets (Eerola and Määttänen, 2013). From this standpoint, a source of distortion in most OECD countries concerns the non-taxation of imputed rents, whereas rental income is taxed. Gervais (2002) and Nakajima (2010) show that this omission has a substantial negative impact on well-being. One of the aims of the the Swiss system of taxing real estate is to achieve tax neutrality by treating the owner-occupier in the same way as the pair formed by the landlord and tenant. This means fully taxing imputed rents after deduction of expenses. The second source of inefficiency may arise from differences in the taxation of property, consumer goods and other assets. This is an important problem, since property represents a substantial proportion of the capital stock in most countries.

In practice, the Swiss system is based on a trade-off between the two constitutional goals of tax neutrality on the one hand and promotion of home ownership on the other hand. This is achieved by taxing imputed rents below-market rates (although not by as much as in some other countries where imputed rents are taxed). As a consequence the taxation of imputed rents in Switzerland generates no net tax revenue. Indeed, a previous study (Peters, 2009) calculated that housing accounts in aggregate are in deficit, so that abolition of the taxation of imputed rents (along with the deductibility of interest payments and maintenance expenses) would actually increase tax revenue although a more recent study suggests it would be revenue neutral, especially given the current low-interest rate environment (Morger, 2014). Another problem is that the system gives homeowners an incentive to maintain large unamortised mortgages and to invest their savings in third-pillar pension funds or other assets which are tax-privileged (in particular, assets which generate tax-exempted capital gains). This creates incentives for holding gross indebtedness at a high level and generates a tax-deductible expense and no extra revenue. Recent rule changes requiring mortgages to be partially amortised have to some extent addressed this issue (see below). The other major source of inflated expenses is that environmental and energy-saving investments are claimed as maintenance expenses. One solution would be to simply disallow claims that exceed the imputed rent tax liability to be written off against other income. Another solution would be to control maintenance expenditures by allowing a fixed charge as a percentage of the value of the building and to treat additional expenditures as capital outlays to be depreciated over time. A solution along these lines was adopted in the Netherlands in 1971, although even so, owner-occupied housing accounts there too remain in deficit by about 2% of GDP; but this is probably related to the generosity of mortgage debt relief rather than to the treatment of deductible expenditures (Vandevyvere and Zenthöfer, 2011).

While phasing out the taxation of imputed rents and all of the associated expense claims including mortgage interest payments might be considered, a careful evaluation must also include incentives on other savings instruments. A pragmatic solution would be to impose a ceiling on expense claims, so deductions cannot exceed taxes paid on imputed rents. As a first step, unless rented out, mortgage interest deductibility should be restricted for owner-occupied and second homes. In any case, deductible expenses should be more strictly defined, particularly the amount of allowable interest deductions, properties should be valued more frequently, and the amount of imputed rental income should be more closely aligned to market levels. And, finally, net deductions from housing should be ring-fenced so that they cannot be applied to other income.

Tenancy law and low rental yields

Rental yields are one of the inputs in the decision to invest in buy-to-let real estate. In Switzerland, nominal rental yields as low as 3% in some cities (Wüest & Partner, 2013) and around 4% for the whole of the country (Figure 1.16) either imply house price overvaluation or may be attributable to rent controls. In Switzerland, tenant protection from abusive rents is a constitutional right. Only apartments that come onto the market for the first time are exempt from rent control and so subject to market forces. In principle, the relationship between the landlord and the tenant is determined by a contractual agreement, and the rent can be freely agreed by the parties. This first tenant can, however, challenge the rent, which can be reviewed for unfair terms.

Figure 1.16. **Rental yields in premier cities in selected OECD countries,[1] mid-2014**

% of market price

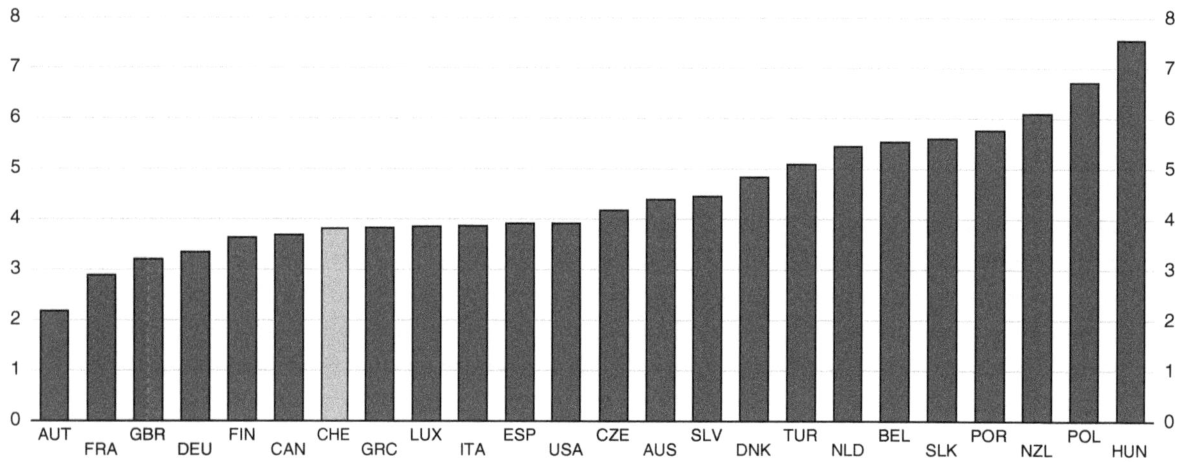

1. The gross annual rental income for 120-sq.m. apartments located in premier city centres, expressed as a percentage of property purchase price before taxes, maintenance fees and other costs.

Source: GlobalPropertyGuide.com.

StatLink http://dx.doi.org/10.1787/888933292592

As soon as the first lease has been signed, tenancy law takes over, and the rent can be adjusted for inflation, the reference interest rate and other cost factors. In spite of the falling reference interest rate, rents for existing tenants have been more or less stable in recent years. Several attempts have been made to uncouple rents from interest rates, but all have failed for political reasons. After the contract ends, the owner can raise the rent for the next tenant to the local market level, which can again be disputed, and the landlord has to prove compliance with the law. One of the parameters considered is the rent prevailing in neighbouring residences. Apart from cases of tenant misbehaviour, the owner can terminate an ongoing contract only if s/he needs the apartment for him/herself or for close relatives, or if the apartment is to be thoroughly renovated. In order to improve transparency in the rental market and to damp rent increases, the Federal Council recently decided that landlords must communicate the previous tenant's rent to potential new tenants. A draft law was presented to the parliament in spring 2015.

In times of high demand for rental apartments, the tenancy laws can lead to market distortions, as market rents increase much faster than ongoing contract rents. Long-term tenants therefore have no incentive to move even if the quality and size of their current apartment surpass their needs. It is usually much more expensive for an elderly couple to move to a new or refurbished smaller dwelling than to stay in their large, depreciated dwelling after their children move out. These lock-in effects temporarily increase statistics on the consumption of floor space per capita, de-densify the population and prolong housing shortages. One solution would be to allow renegotiation of rents after the end of the term of a contract, rather than only when the tenant changes. Consideration should also be given to applying differentiated rent-setting rules when large residences are occupied by few people, although such a formula should take into account the ability of low-income households to pay for moving. Moreover, broader deregulation of the tenancy laws would possibly lead to higher rents, harming low-income groups. To support them, targeted housing allowances and/or more social housing would be needed.

Non-profit co-operatives and social housing

Social housing comprises a very small proportion of the Swiss dwelling stock with only around 14% of rental properties in this category. This is among the lowest shares in the OECD – far below that of the Netherlands, Austria, and the Nordic countries, although on a par with Germany and Luxembourg (Figure 1.5). In Switzerland many of these dwellings are provided by non-governmental, non-profit co-operatives that let their apartments at cost. Most co-operatives operate in large cities, where affordable housing is most needed because of high rents and the large number of poorer households (Table 1.1). While some co-operatives operate totally independently from government and impose few restrictions on their tenants (as to household income or persons per dwelling), most receive some form of subsidy, such as land for building and leases at below-market prices, tax breaks and financing at below-market interest rates. These subsidies usually come with an obligation to let the units only to low-income households. Some co-operatives impose some form of redistribution within the co-operative where households with higher incomes subsidise low-income households to some extent.

Table 1.1. **Apartments owned by non-profit co-operatives, 2013**

	Number	% of total number of apartments
Switzerland	157 564	3.7
Zurich	40 637	18.9
Geneva	4 785	4.5
Basel	9 517	9.9
Bern	5 298	6.9
Lausanne	5 463	7.3

Source: Swiss Federal Housing Office.

Until a few years ago most local and regional authorities had no explicit policies with regard to affordable housing. Since then voters in several cantons and municipalities have passed initiatives forcing governments to adopt a strategic approach and to increase its supply. Voters in the Canton of Zurich and the city of Zug, for example, want their respective governments to establish planning zones where at least part of any newly built floor space is dedicated to affordable housing. To counter the shortage of affordable housing, the canton of Geneva passed a law obliging new buildings in a *zone de développement* to have a minimum percentage of subsidised apartments or part of the building to belong permanently to the government or a non-profit organisation that will manage subsidised housing (Credit Suisse, 2014). In spite of this law, the Geneva cantonal government's 2007 goal of 3 500 additional subsidised apartments per year has so far been missed by a wide margin, with only 1 400 units built per year on average, of which only around 500 are subsidised (République et Canton de Genève, 2015).

Macroeconomic risks from the housing market

At the end of 2013 there were 283 banks in Switzerland: 2 big banks (Credit Suisse and UBS), 24 cantonal banks (the biggest being Banque Cantonale Vaudoise and Zürcher Kantonalbank), 64 regional banks and savings banks, Raiffeisen bank (comprising 305 co-operatives), 47 stock exchange banks, 14 other banking institutions, 93 foreign-controlled banks, 27 branches of foreign banks and 11 private banks. These numbers have remained roughly constant over the past decade, except for regional banks and savings banks where the consolidation that began in the aftermath of the bursting of the 1980s housing bubble and subsequent banking crisis (Box 1.3) has continued, albeit at a much more measured pace.

Banks that are exposed to the real estate sector through mortgage lending are subject to both interest-rate and house-price risks. Direct interest-rate risk arises when there is a mismatch between the interest rate at which a bank borrows and that at which it lends, whereas indirect interest-rate risk captures the risk that borrowers become unable to pay as interest rates rise. House-price risk arises when the value of the house falls below the value of the mortgage used to purchase the property. Internally, banks handle these risks through asset and liability management (ALM) strategies. But because of the potentially large negative externalities of bank failures, governments task prudential supervisory agencies with regulating mortgage lenders to ensure these risks are being properly managed.

In Switzerland, this prudential supervision is jointly handled by the SNB and the Financial Market Supervisory Authority (FINMA). The Federal Department of Finance (FDF) also plays a role, particularly in so far as the Federal Council needs to be involved. To facilitate these joint supervisory and regulatory roles, MOUs were signed between the SNB and FINMA in 2007 (and revised in 2010 to establish a Steering Committee, which is responsible for co-operation between the two institutions at strategic level), and between the SNB, FINMA and the FDF in 2011; the latter governs collaboration among the three authorities, including the exchange of information on financial stability and financial market regulation issues, as well as collaboration in the event of a crisis. Legislation is currently being drafted aimed at strengthening information exchange among them.

In the current instance, where mortgage interest rates are at historic lows and house prices are at historic highs, the risk to the banking sector is higher than the norm of the past few decades. In contrast to most other European countries, the exposure of Swiss banks to residential real estate has increased substantially over the past five years, with the ratio of the stock of residential loans to total bank loans increasing from 30% in 2009 to 38% in 2013 (Figure 1.17, Panel A). SNB data shows that mortgages make up around 84% of all domestic bank loans excluding interbank credit. With a stock of residential real estate loans at over 120% of GDP, Switzerland is the leader in the OECD (Panel B). Indeed, interest-rate risk has become more acute in Switzerland in recent years as more and more borrowers take fixed-rate mortgages, typically fixed for five to ten years, and also because the interest rate on mortgages has dropped so dramatically in recent years. Already in 2013 around 15% of new mortgages bore an interest rate of less than 0.5%.

Box 1.3. **The 1990s Swiss banking crisis**

The strong real estate market boom during the 1980s saw the stock of domestic mortgages double between 1981 and 1989. During this time amortisation was not mandatory for the majority of mortgages, and banks typically tolerated high lending limits, with loan-to-value ratios of 80-100% being common. The average ratio of outstanding mortgages to total bank assets was about 30%, with a peak of 36% in 1991. The sharp decline in real estate prices that started in 1989 in the most inflated regions, combined with a general macroeconomic slowdown, adversely affected banks' loan portfolios and some banks started to feel pressures on both sides of their balance sheets. On the assets side, borrowers began to have trouble servicing their debts, especially small businesses and households. Falling real estate prices and high lending limits implied that in many cases the collateral no longer covered the total amount of the mortgage or the loan, and banks were forced to write off large sums. On the liabilities side, banks faced mounting problems to finance their mortgages with savings deposits, forcing some banks to issue medium-term notes and mortgage bonds, although a gradual withdrawal of this type of funding was observed as customers shifted to regular bonds, equities and mutual funds.

Between 1991 and 1996, banks incurred estimated losses of around CHF 42 billion (roughly 8.5% of the total loan volume or more than 10% of annual GDP). A key feature of the Swiss banking system at the time was the high degree of segmentation – there were 371 banks operating in Switzerland at end-2001, of which 219 were domestic banks. While the large banks incurred the biggest share of total losses, their well-diversified portfolios allowed sufficient profits to be earned out of their other businesses to cover these losses. They were strong enough to write off the non-performing loans quickly. Likewise the Raiffeisen banks were not saddled with a significant problem of non-performing loans and therefore emerged relatively unscathed by the crisis. In contrast, the regional and cantonal banks, which focused on the domestic loan business, suffered most. The regional banks bore the brunt of the crisis, with almost half of all them disappearing during that period. However, only a single bank had to be liquidated – in October 1991, the Swiss Federal Banking Commission (SFBC) closed Spar+Leihkasse Thun, a medium-sized regional bank with assets of CHF 1.1 billion. The liquidation was accompanied by depositor losses, as the bank's assets could not cover outstanding liabilities. All other regional banks that experienced problems merged with stronger banks. Five state-owned cantonal banks received taxpayers' money, but the fiscal cost of resolution for these cantonal banks combined was less than 1% of annual Swiss GDP.

As a response to the regional banking crisis, the SFBC introduced an Early Information System in 1997 that allowed it to monitor in real time important balance-sheet ratios, the profit and loss account, off-balance-sheet activities and bad loans. The Swiss National Bank (SNB) created a Systemic Stability division in 2001 and started to co-ordinate the collection of statistical data with the SFBC. As a result of the crisis, a new law on bank insolvency was passed in 2003, which facilitated more efficient liquidation and restructuring of troubled banks and offered better protection for small depositors.

Source: BIS (2004), "Bank Failures in Mature Economies", *Bank for International Settlements Working Paper*, No. 13, April, Basel.

Despite repeated SNB warnings, banks keep expanding their mortgage loan books. In its latest *Financial Stability Report* (SNB, 2015), the SNB stated that banks' risk appetite in mortgage lending remains high overall. While the growth in mortgage lending slowed in 2014 relative to the previous couple of years, at around 4% per annum it still outstripped nominal per capita GDP and disposable income growth. And the historically high level of interest-rate risk in the banking books has not declined.

Figure 1.17. **Stock of residential loans relative to total bank loans and GDP**

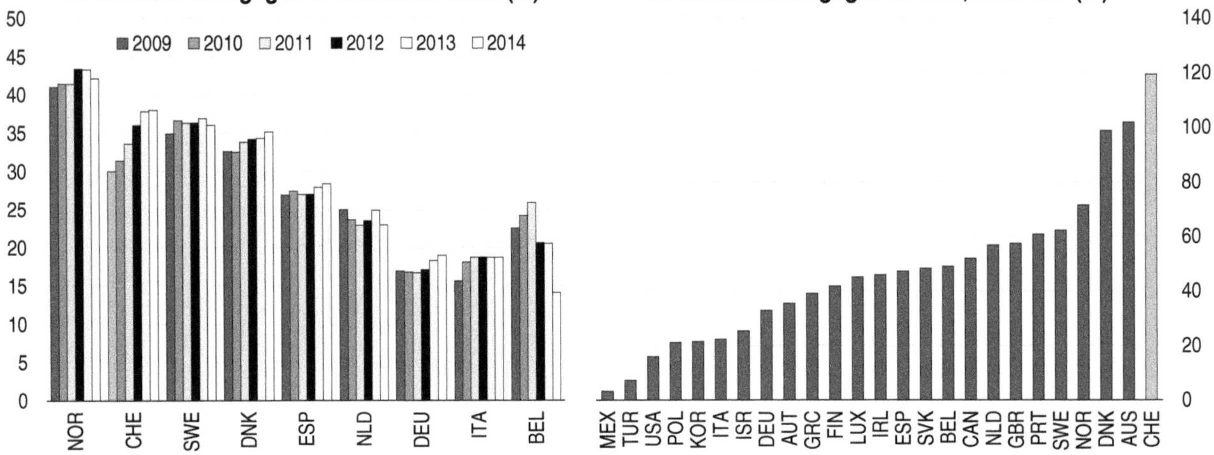

1. Or latest available observation. 2014 annual average for Switzerland.

Source: IMF, *Financial Soundness Indicators* (FSI); *OECD Economic Outlook 97 Database* (and updates); and OECD calculations.

StatLink http://dx.doi.org/10.1787/888933292607

There is considerable variation across bank types in Switzerland in their degree of exposure to the mortgage market. In terms of their shares of the total stock of domestic mortgages, at the beginning of 2015 cantonal banks were the largest players, having just over a third, while the two big banks held around 29% (Figure 1.18, Panel A). Reflecting ongoing consolidation among regional and savings banks, their share has declined over the past three decades to around 10%, while the share of Raiffeisen and other banks has increased from below 5% in 1990 to 24% at the beginning of 2015 (Box 1.4). According to Raiffeisen Schweiz figures, the group's share of the total Swiss mortgage market was 16.6% at end-2014, up from 12.6% in 2002. The profile of mortgage-to-asset ratios across bank types in Switzerland has remained fairly stable over the past 10 years (Panel B). Regional and savings banks are the most mortgage-focused, with around 80% of their assets in

Figure 1.18. **Total mortgage loans by bank type**

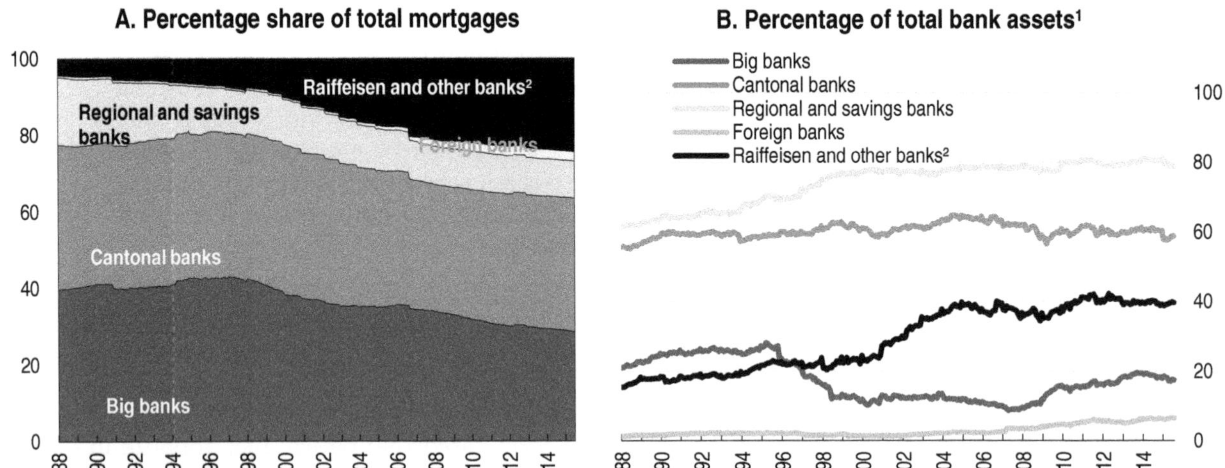

1. Domestic mortgages as a percentage of total foreign and domestic assets.
2. Excluding PostFinance.

Source: SNB (2015), *Monthly Bulletin of Banking Statistics*, September.

StatLink http://dx.doi.org/10.1787/888933292614

Box 1.4. One hundred years of Raiffeisen banks in Switzerland

Raiffeisen Group is a Swiss co-operative bank. After UBS and Credit Suisse, it is the third largest bank in Switzerland. Raiffeisen has 3.7 million customers, 1.8 million of whom are co-operative members (co-owners). The Group consists of the 305 co-operatively structured banks, which collectively have over one thousand branches throughout Switzerland and around 11 000 employees. The group is a member of the International Raiffeisen Union (IRU), which is an association of co-operatives based on the ideas of Friedrich Wilhelm Raiffeisen (1818-88). Switzerland's first Raiffeisen bank was founded in Bichelsee, Canton Thurgau, a century ago. The purpose of the initiative, taken by a local clergyman, was to ease the dire financial position of the farming and business community by letting the people help themselves.

The size of the group has more than doubled over the past 14 years, and mortgage loans have increased by around 120% over that period (Table 1.2). Its share of the domestic mortgage market has increased from 12.5% in 2002 to 16.6% in 2014. The success of the Raiffeisen is based on several factors. First, the granting of loan facilities is limited to low-risk commitments to members of the individual banks. The fact that borrowers must be co-owners who are liable to provide additional cover makes borrowing unattractive for high-risk customers. On an organisational level, there is a combination of decentralised responsibility of the member banks with the strong management role of the St. Gallen head office. The latter plays a vital role in monitoring business activity and undertaking structural adjustments.

Table 1.2. Raiffeisen Group balance sheet and mortgage share

	Assets CHF mlns	**Mortgages** CHF mlns	**Mortgage to asset ratio** %	**Percentage of domestic mortgage market** %
2002	92 684	68 570	74.0	12.5
2005	108 187	83 893	77.5	13.8
2010	147 239	119 595	81.2	15.7
2013	176 575	143 659	81.4	16.3
2014	188 640	150 880	80.0	16.6

Source: *Raiffeisen Group Annual Reports*, various editions.

Over the past three years, Moody's has downgraded its rating of Raiffeisen Group from Aa1 to Aa3. The most recent downgrade, in July 2013, was instigated by: i) the Group's above-average residential mortgage-loan growth over recent years, leading to increased susceptibility to shocks under a scenario of a significant slowdown in the Swiss housing market; and ii) the continued challenging operating environment, characterised by net interest margin compression and low interest rates, which constrain the group's profitability prospects.

mortgages. For cantonal banks the ratio is around 60% and for Raiffeisen around 80%, and other banks around 40%. The big banks have seen some increase in asset concentration in mortgages, going from 10% in 2007 to close to 20% in 2015; however, this is largely a reflection of a consolidation in the business of the two big banks since the global financial crisis and the Too-Big-To-Fail (TBTF) reforms, which sought to address systemic risk arising from Switzerland's large financial institutions including from moral hazard.

Prudential measures in the mortgage market

Switzerland's prudential regulation of its mortgage lenders is a combination of legal directives by supervisory authorities and self-regulation by the banking industry. Table 1.3 outlines the array of legal requirements, banking industry guidelines and individual bank internal policies. Self-regulation plays a very important role, although sometimes arm-twisting by the authorities has been required, and, indeed, self-regulatory measures adopted by the banking sector typically receive the imprimatur of the regulatory authorities. These self-regulations are not mandatory, and, indeed, mortgages that breach these guidelines are not uncommon these days. Self-regulations where minimum standards are not fulfilled, are rather uncommon. In these cases, the entire mortgage amount must be risk weighted at 100%. The second prong of regulation is legal directives that are imposed by the supervisory authorities including the Federal Council, SNB and FINMA.

Table 1.3. **Regulation and "self" regulation in the mortgage sector**

Regulations/Policies	Regime	Date
Borrowers required to provide at least 10% in equity (excluding second-pillar pension savings) when applying for a new mortgage.	FINMA-approved self-regulation (of the SBA)[1]	July 2012 (5-month transition period)
The mortgage must be amortised to an LTV of two-thirds within 20 years.	FINMA-approved self-regulation (of the SBA)[1]	July 2012 (5-month transition period)
The legal framework for a counter-cyclical capital buffer (CCB) was put in place.	Legal	July 2012
The SNB abstained from proposing the activation of the CCB for the mortgage sector.	Legal	August 2012
Increase in capital requirements for high-LTV loans.	Legal	January 2013
Sectoral CCB activated. Set at 1% by 30th September 2013 (announced in February 2013).	Legal	February 2013
Sectoral CCB raised to 2% by 30th June 2014 (announced in January 2014).	Legal	January 2014
New mortgages must be amortised to a LTV of two-thirds within 15 years, subject to linear repayment.	FINMA-approved self-regulation (of the SBA)[1]	September 2014 (5-month transition period)
General and qualitative guidelines of the Swiss Bankers Association (SBA)		
First revision of the guidelines of the Swiss Bankers Association "on examining, evaluating and settling mortgage-backed loans". Issues covered, among other things, are affordability (methods for calculation of a level of sustainable income), property valuation standards, loan-to-value, and amortisation.	FINMA-approved self-regulation (of the SBA)	October 2011
Second revision of the guidelines of the Swiss Bankers Association "on examining, evaluating and settling mortgage-backed loans". Focus on second incomes and the "lower of cost or market" principle. (This was coupled with the shortening of the amortisation period which is implemented as a minimum standard).	FINMA-approved self-regulation (of the SBA)	September 2014
Common internal bank policies		
Loan-to-value of around 80%.		
Interest-to-income (affordability based on imputed interest rates) of around one third.		
Interest rate used in imputing interest payments (5% plus 1% amortisation and 1% of property value for maintenance = appox.7%).		

1. These regulations have the nature of minimum standards within the self-regulation guidelines. Due to competition laws, banks are allowed to circumvent these requirements if they risk weight the entire loan amount with 100%. This treatment is laid down in the Capital Adequacy Ordinance (CAO). For instance, for residential mortgage loans, this would result in a substantial increase compared to an average risk weight of 35% to 50% depending on the LTV.

Source: SBVg (2014), "Richtlinien betreffend Mindestanforderungen bei Hypothekarfinanzierungen", Basel; FINMA; SNB.

While maximum loan-to-value (LTV) ratios for mortgages are not legally binding, the internal polices of banks typically specify a ceiling of 80%. Moreover, high-LTV mortgages are legally required to be backed by high levels of capital, and in January 2013 this rule was tightened further. Guidelines of the Swiss Bankers Association (SBA), which have been approved by FINMA, set down standards for estimating property valuations used in LTV-ratio calculations. With regards to affordability (debt-service coverage) ratios, banks also have internal policies that typically set a target of no more than one-third. However, unlike LTV ratios, there are no legal regulations dealing with affordability, only SBA guidelines for the calculation of a level of sustainable income. Moreover, banks' practice of using a 5% interest rate (a long-term historical average), with 1% for amortisation costs and 1% of the total property value for maintenance costs added on top, to calculate an affordability ratio, gives a large precautionary buffer in the current environment of historically low mortgage interest rates.

Estimates put the average LTV ratio in the Swiss housing market at about 45%. This may seem low, but it reflects the fact that a substantial share of households has little or no debt, as they have already repaid almost all of their mortgages. This means that many new home owners have a much higher LTV ratio. The share of new mortgage loans with a LTV exceeding 80% has declined in the last two years, but still one in six new mortgages exceeds the threshold, notably based on a most likely "overheated" property value (Figure 1.19, Panel A).

However, from the point of view of the banks, they tend to be more sanguine regarding the risks, taking the view that, even if they have trouble repaying mortgages, most borrowers have scope to cut discretionary spending, such as for holidays and other consumption, in order to not default and remain home owners (see below). Therefore, an

Figure 1.19. **Share of new mortgages with high loan-to-value and implied debt-service-to-income ratios**

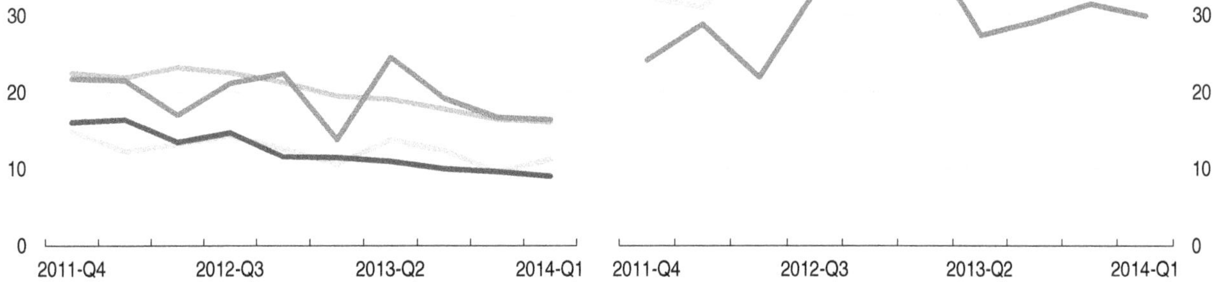

1. Proportion of new mortgages with LTVs above 80%.
2. Proportion of new mortgages with LTIs where imputed costs would exceed one-third of gross wage or pension income (private properties) or rental income (investment properties), respectively, at an interest rate of 5% as well as 1% for maintenance costs and 1% for amortisation costs.
3. Net figures including pledges from pillar 2 and 3a pension funds.

Source: SNB (2014), *Financial Stability Report 2014*, Zurich.

StatLink http://dx.doi.org/10.1787/888933292418

excessive LTV would be a minor problem as long as the borrower could pay the interest, and therefore the debt-service-to-income ratio should be the primary focus. Interestingly, however, recent regulation and "self" regulation have concentrated on appropriate LTV ratios and not on the debt-service-to-income ratio. Banks are free to set their own policy in this regard. In its *Financial Stability Report 2015*, SNB (2015) calculated that the proportion of new mortgages for owner-occupied residential real estate that exceed the one-third interest-to-income ratio was 41% in 2014 when applying a 5% interest rate and current disposable income levels as the base (Figure 1.19, Panel B). Consideration should be given to formulating a framework for explicitly regulating affordability with a view to adding this to the macro-prudential toolkit. Moreover, given that borrowers financing rental properties may not be as responsive as households' borrowing to recent regulatory measures, mortgage lending to these borrowers should be monitored closely.

In June 2012, the Federal Council agreed to implement a package of measures aimed at reducing risks in the housing market, including the so-called counter-cyclical buffer (CCB). Its two main objectives are, first, to protect the banking sector from the consequences of excessive credit growth by increasing its loss-absorbing capacity and, second, to reduce the attractiveness of mortgage lending. The CCB is a component of the Basel III framework and is to be introduced by most countries over the next few years. It was introduced early in Switzerland following concerns about the risks of cyclical imbalances developing in the domestic mortgage and real estate markets. The CCB framework has been implemented so that it can be applied on a broad basis or targeted at specific segments of the credit market. Also, in line with Basel III, the maximum level of the CCB is set at 2.5% of total domestic risk-weighted assets of the individual bank. The CCB is applicable to Swiss banks and to subsidiaries of foreign banks. Activation and adjustments to the CCB are proposed to the Federal Council by the SNB after consultations with the FINMA. It is the Federal Council that takes the final decision on the CCB, and FINMA supervises its implementation at the individual bank level.

The CCB was first activated in February 2013, with the Federal Council accepting the SNB's request to require banks to increase capital by 1% of their residential-mortgage lending by September 2013. In January 2014, the CCB was increased to 2%, with required compliance by end-June 2014. The SNB decided that it was necessary to increase the CCB because, while the initial activation boosted banks' resilience, the sustained strong increase in mortgage loans and the prices of residential properties caused imbalances to continue to build up in the low-interest-rate environment. It was the SNB's assessment that these imbalances constituted a considerable risk for the stable development of the economy and thus also for the banking sector's soundness.

Risks to households

Measured in gross terms, Swiss households are among the most indebted in the OECD and have become more so over the past decade (Figure 1.20). In 2013 gross household debt in Switzerland reached 200% of household disposable income. Moreover, according to SNB data, in 2013 mortgages made up over 92% of all household financial liabilities and between 2000 and 2013 the total stock of mortgages held by Swiss households increased by 66%, while all other financial liabilities increased by just 5%. As seen above, the Swiss tax system generates incentives for households to leverage their wealth. The deductibility of mortgage interest payments is both regressive and encourages borrowing, and the wealth

Figure 1.20. **Household debt in OECD countries**

% of disposable income

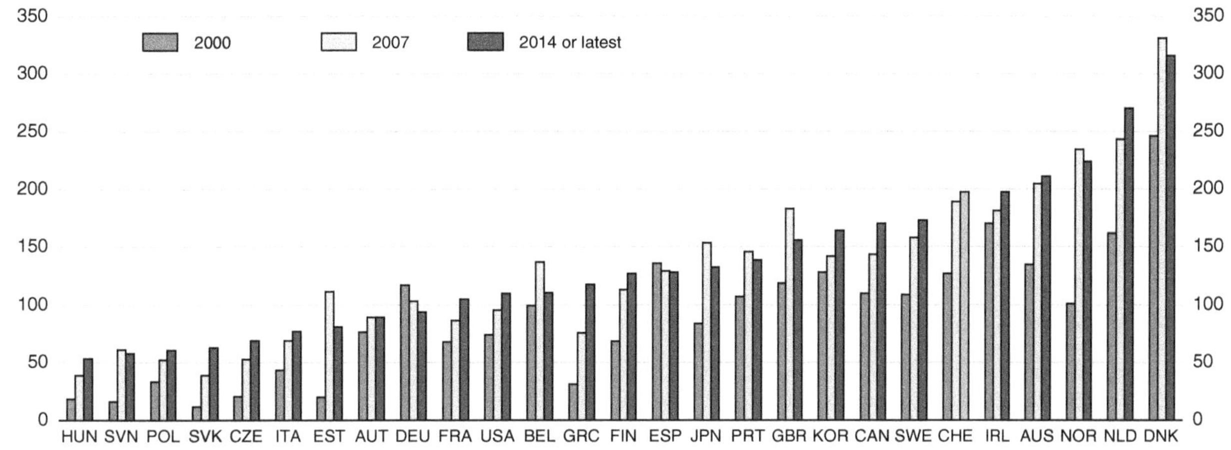

Source: *OECD Economic Outlook 97 Database* (and updates) and national sources.

StatLink http://dx.doi.org/10.1787/888933292629

tax does not diminish incentives to leverage, as it is assessed on net household wealth. Jordà et al. (2014) show that the severity of economic downturns is related to the level of household debt, suggesting the importance of focusing macro-prudential policy on the vulnerabilities inherent in high levels of household debt.

Overall, the ability of many households to weather an adverse macroeconomic shock or a major change in interest rates is questionable. It is comforting that, contrary to the situation in the early 1990s, most mortgages granted in the last 10 years are at fixed interest rates, which are thought to temporarily shield the borrowers against the effects of rising interest rates. Nevertheless, the maturity structure of said mortgages gives reason for concern, as 75% of total mortgage volume will have to be re-priced in the next five years, with roughly 40% of the stock maturing within 12 months (SNB, 2015). A major part of the domestic mortgage volume will thus be affected by interest rate changes in the short and medium term. That said, a substantial buffer against household default is provided by banks' practice of using an indicative interest rate significantly higher than current market rate when assessing a household's eligibility for a mortgage. Nevertheless, as pointed out above, a large share of mortgages breaches this self-regulation, particularly with regard to interest-to-income ratios. Nonetheless, Brown and Guin (2013) concluded that if interest rates went back to their long-term level of 5% and house prices adjusted downwards by 20%, this would not, in the short or medium term, lead to a significant increase in mortgage defaults. However, if this situation were sustained, as happened in Switzerland in the 1990s, it could result in a significant increase in mortgage defaults. The SNB also warned of this possible outcome in its 2014 *Financial Stability Report* (SNB, 2014). That having been said, recent research suggests that highly indebted households are willing to cut consumption more than less indebted households in the event of a crisis, suggesting resilience in the face of possible mortgage default (Baker, 2014; Bunn 2014; Lau Andersen et al., 2014).

Recommendations to mitigate risks in the housing market

- Establish a framework for explicitly addressing affordability risk, to be used if needed to contain financial stability risks related to imbalances in the housing and mortgage markets. Reassess the role played by government-mandated guaranteed returns on pension funds in fuelling the boom in house prices.
- Review spatial planning regulations to make it easier to build denser housing.
- Undertake audits of potential for added value in existing dwellings, and provide this information to homeowners.
- Harmonise cantonal and communal land-use and building codes to promote greater competition and economies of scale in the construction industry.
- Adjust tenancy law to minimise lock-in effects.
- Adjust the valuation of properties used in calculating imputed rental income more frequently so that it more closely follows market prices.
- Limit the tax deductibility of mortgage interest so that, combined with maintenance outlays, it does not exceed to the amount of declared imputed rent.
- Impose an extra tax on land in high-demand areas that has been rezoned for real estate but has remained undeveloped for more than five years.
- Restrict income tax privileges or mortgage deductibility for owner-occupied first and second-home owners.
- Ensure that the SNB and other regulators continue their communication strategy of warning households and investors of the growing risks of borrowing to purchase real estate.
- Monitor closely mortgage lending to firms or households for rental properties, which may not be as responsive as the owner-occupied segment to recent regulatory measures.

Bibliography

Andrews, D. and A. Caldera Sánchez (2011), "The Evolution of Homeownership Rates in Selected OECD Countries: Demographic and Public Policy Influences", *OECD Journal: Economic Studies*, Vol. 2011/1, OECD Publishing.

Andrews, D., A. Caldera Sánchez and Å. Johansson (2011), "Housing Markets and Structural Policies in OECD Countries", *OECD Economics Department Working Papers*, No. 836, OECD Publishing.

ARE (2014a), "Revision des Raumplanungsgesetzes (RPG) – 1. Etappe", Federal office for spatial development, Ittigen, *www.are.admin.ch/themen/recht/04651/index.html?lang=de*.

ARE (2014b), "Zweite Etappe der Revision des Raumplanungsgesetzes: Vernehmlassung eröffnet", Federal office for spatial development, Ittigen, *www.are.admin.ch/dokumentation/00121/00224/index.html?lang=de&msg-id=55541*.

Aregger, H., M. Brown and E. Rossi (2013), "Transaction Taxes, Capital Gains Taxes and House Prices", *Swiss National Bank Working Papers*, No. 2013-2.

Baker, S.R. (2014), "Debt and the Consumption Response to Household Income Shocks", *SSRN Research Paper*, No. 2541142.

BIS (2004), "Bank Failures in Mature Economics", *Bank for International Settlements Working Paper*, No. 13, April, Bank for International Settlements, Basel.

BIS (2013), "Regulatory Consistency Assessment Programme: Assessment of Basel III regulations – Switzerland", Bank for International Settlements, Basel.

Blöchliger, H., B. Egert, B. Alvarez and A. Paciorek (2015), "The Stabilising Properties of Immovable Property Taxation: Evidence from OECD Countries", *OECD Economics Department Working Papers*, forthcoming, OECD Publishing.

Bourassa, S. and M. Hoesli (2006), "Why Do the Swiss Rent?", *Swiss Finance Institute Research Paper*, No. 07-04, 27 December.

Bourassa, S. and M. Hoesli (2010), "Why Do the Swiss Rent?", *Journal of Real Estate Finance and Economics*, Vol. 40, No. 3, pp. 286-309.

Bourassa, S., M. Hoesli and D. Scognamiglio (2010), "Housing finance, prices, and tenure in Switzerland", *MPRA Paper*, No. 45990.

Brown, M. and B. Guin (2013), "How Risky are Residential Mortgages in Switzerland?", *University of St. Gallen Working Paper*, Swiss Institute of Banking and Finance, 6 December.

BSV (2014), "Richtungsentscheid für eine Reform der Ergänzungsleistungen", Federal social insurance office, Bern.

Bunn, P. (2014), "Household debt and spending", *Quarterly Bulletin*, 2014 Q3, Bank of England, London.

Caldera Sánchez, A. and Å. Johansson (2013), "The price responsiveness of housing supply in OECD countries", *Journal of Housing Economics*, Volume 22, Issue 3, pp. 231-49, September.

Carey, D., K. Gordon and P. Thalmann (1999) "Tax Reform in Switzerland", *OECD Economics Department Working Papers*, No. 222, OECD Publishing.

Credit Suisse (2014), "Immomonitor 2Q 2014", Zurich.

Credit Suisse (2015), "Real Estate Market 2015. Structures and Prospects", March, Zurich.

Eerola, E. and N. Määttänen (2013), "The Optimal Tax Treatment of Housing Capital in the Neoclassical Growth Model", *Journal of Public Economic Theory*, Vol. 15, No. 6, pp. 912-38.

Evans, A. and O. Hartwich (2005), "Bigger Better Faster More: why some countries plan better than others", *Policy Exchange*, London.

Fahrländer, S. (2007), "Hedonische Immobilienbewertung: Eine empirische Untersuchung der Schweizer Märkte für Wohneigentum 1985 bis 2005", Munich.

Fahrländer Partner (2008), "Bauzonen Schweiz: Wie viele Bauzonen braucht die Schweiz?", Ed. Federal Office of Bundesamt für Raumentwicklung ARE, Ittigen.

Fahrländer Partner (2014), "Immobilien-Preisindizes von Fahrländer Partner: Methoden-Kurzbeschrieb", Zurich.

Fahrländer Partner and sotomo (2014), "Segmentation of Demand in the Housing Market: Methodological Description", Zurich.

Gervais, M. (2002), "Housing taxation and capital accumulation", *Journal of Monetary Economics*, Vol. 49, No. 7, pp. 1461-89.

Hott, C. and T. Jokipii (2012), "Housing Bubbles and Interest Rates", *Working Papers*, No. 2012-07, Swiss National Bank.

IMF (2014), "Switzerland: Technical Note – Macroprudential Institutional Arrangements and Policies", Washington, DC.

Jordà, Ò., M. Schularick and A. Taylor (2014), "The Great Mortgaging: Housing Finance, Crises and Business Cycles", *NBER Working Papers*, No. 20501.

Koźluk, T. (2014), "The Indicators of the Economic Burdens of Environmental Policy Design: Results from the OECD Questionnaire", *OECD Economics Department Working Papers*, No. 1178, OECD Publishing.

Kugler, P. and C. Lenz (2001), "Capital gains taxation: evidence from Switzerland", *International Evidence on the Effects of Having No Capital Gains Taxes*, Fraser Institute, Vancouver.

Lau Andersen, A., C. Duus and T. L. Jensen (2014), "Household debt and consumption during the financial crisis: Evidence from Danish micro data", *Danmarks Nationalbank Working Papers*, No. 2014-89, Copenhagen.

Liebig, T., S. Kohls and K. Krause (2012), "The labour market integration of immigrants and their children in Switzerland", *OECD Social, Employment and Migration Working Papers* No. 128, OECD Publishing.

Morger, M. (2014), "Eigenmietwertbesteuerung: Anreizmechanismen, Verteilungseffekte und finanzielle Auswirkungen verschiedener Reform-optionen", Eidgenössische Steuerverwaltung ESTV, Abteilung Grundlagen.

Nakajima, M. (2010), "Optimal Capital Income Taxation with Housing", *Federal Reserve Bank of Philadelphia Working Paper*, No. 10-11.

Neff, M. and P. Rauh (2005), "Spotlight: Immobilienblase in der Schweiz?", Ed. Credit Suisse, Zurich.

NZZ (2005), "Keine Immobilienblase in der Schweiz: Lokal deutliche Preissteigerungen bei Eigenheimen", *Neue Zürcher Zeitung*, No. 285, p. 25, 6 December.

OECD (2009), *OECD Economic Surveys: Switzerland 2009*, OECD Publishing.

OECD (2011), *How's life? Measuring wellbeing 2011*, OECD Publishing.

OECD (2013), *OECD Economic Surveys: Switzerland 2013*, OECD Publishing.

OECD (2014), *OECD Better Life Index 2014*, OECD Publishing.

OECD (2015), *Indicators of Migrant Integration 2015: Settling In*, OECD Publishing.

Peters, R. (2009), "Les déductions de l'imposition fédérale directe des personnes physiques et les possibilités de simplification : Une analyse des données fiscales du canton de Berne année 2005", Administration fédérale des contributions AFC.

Plank, M. (2012), "Basel III and its implication on the financial industry", ETH risk day, Zurich.

République et Canton de Genève (2015), "Statistique du parc immobilier", Office cantonal de la statistique, Geneva.

Salvi, M. and J. Syz (20011), "What Drives 'Green Housing' Construction? Evidence from Switzerland", *Journal of Financial Economic Policy*, Vol. 3, No. 1, pp. 86-102.

SBA (2014), "Richtlinien für die Prüfung, Bewertung und Abwicklung grundpfandgesicherter Kredite", Swiss Banking Association, Basel.

SNB (2014), *Financial Stability Report 2014*, Swiss National Bank, Zurich.

SNB (2015), *Financial Stability Report 2015*, Swiss National Bank, Zurich.

Steiner, E. (2010), "Estimating a stock-flow model of the Swiss housing market", *Swiss National Bank Working Papers*, No. 2010-8, Swiss National Bank.

Thalmann, P. (2012), "Housing market equilibrium (almost) without vacancies", *Urban Studies*, Vol. 49, No. 8, June.

UBS (2014), "Einschränkung des Kapitalbezugs aus der beruflichen Vorsorge", Zurich.

Vandevyvere, W., and A. Zenthöfer (2011), "The housing market in the Netherlands", *European Economy Economic Papers*, No. 457.

Wehrmüller, A. (2014), "TENLAW: Tenancy Law and Housing Policy in Multi-level Europe – National Report for Switzerland", European Commission.

Zürcher Kantonalbank (2010), "Immigration 2030", Zurich.

Chapter 2

Raising public spending efficiency

Despite having low government spending, Switzerland scores highly in various public policy outcomes, including health, education and transportation. But, as the population grows and ages, efficiency of public spending will have to rise to maintain low tax rates. Given its high returns, the provision of early childhood education and care should be boosted, especially for children from disadvantaged socio-economic backgrounds, including those from immigrant families. Cantons should avoid oversupplying baccalaureates, thereby lowering university dropout rates. Policies will also need to adapt to structural changes in the labour market, by boosting the supply and attractiveness of fields of study that are facing high demand on the labour market, and by further clarifying study streams across tertiary education. Health-care efficiency could be raised by further developing managed-care networks. Enforcing systematic data collection for the quality of care would also help patients and providers make better informed choices. Generic drugs' prices are too high due to a poorly designed price-fixing mechanism. Transportation suffers from congestion that could be reduced by implementing peak-load pricing on roads and trains. But efficiency in public spending is also about allocating public funds optimally. Switzerland's rapidly rising social security entitlements and its fiscal equalisation system constrain public spending and risk crowding out important expenditures. Fast-rising social security entitlements could be addressed via indexing the retirement age to life expectancy. Fiscal equalisation weakens tax-raising incentives for some cantons; this could be addressed by allowing them to keep a larger part of their increased revenues. Efficiency in allocating public expenditure could also be raised by increasing the share of public spending allocated by tender and harmonising procurement regulations across all levels of government.

Introduction

Public expenditure in Switzerland was just 33.5% of GDP in 2014, a share that has remained largely unchanged over the past decade and a half (Figure 2.1, Panel A). Likewise, the share of public employment is very low (Panel B). The small size of the public sector is a reflection of a long-standing and well entrenched ethos of fiscal conservatism and a limited role for government, where both the cantons (since the 1990s) and the Confederation (since 2001) have been subject to so-called debt-brake and other budget rules that hold down expenditures and the deficit.

The relatively low level of public expenditure has been no obstacle to Switzerland's high international ranking on several public policy outcomes. For instance, at 82.9 years, it enjoys the second highest life expectancy at birth in Europe, after Iceland (EUROSTAT, 2015). It had the highest mathematics score among non-Asian nations in the 2012 PISA evaluation and ranked fifth overall (OECD, 2014f). It also has the most kilometres of railroad track per square kilometre and per person. Its judicial performance is impressive too, with the shortest trial length of 31 OECD countries (Palumbo et al., 2013).

Figure 2.1. **Government spending and employment**

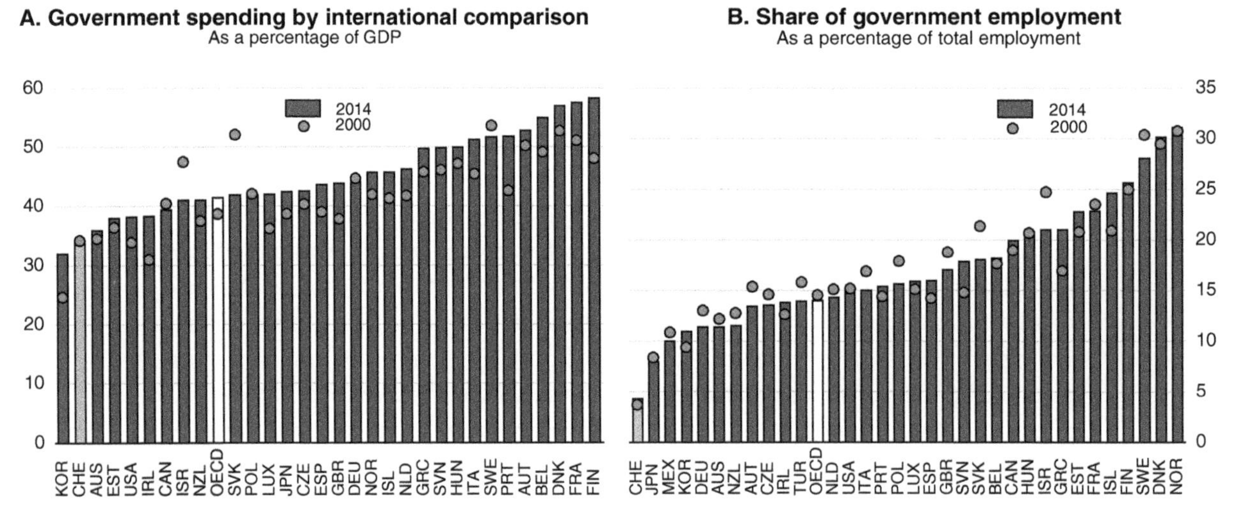

Source: *OECD, Economic Outlook No. 97 Database* (and updates).

StatLink http://dx.doi.org/10.1787/888933292634

Nevertheless, the country faces a number of pressures that will require more spending or a still more efficient public sector. As in most OECD countries, the falling ratio of workers to retirees is putting pressure on the old-age pension system. And the rise in life expectancy and chronic medical conditions are already pushing up health expenditures, especially for long-term care. If current growth rates for social and health-care spending were to continue, they would absorb 70% of all public expenditure in 2030, versus 38%

today (économiesuisse, 2012). At the same time, a growing and increasingly complex economy will require developing and improving the transportation network, and productivity gains will need an increasingly educated workforce to be sustained. Both of these will put greater demands on public spending.

Evaluating the efficiency of public expenditure can be done using a technique known as Data Envelopment Analysis (DEA). The idea is to compare a country's outcomes in a particular area of public policy with that of the best performing countries. Performance is measured in terms of output efficiency (e.g. PISA scores) and input efficiency (e.g. education spending or class size) (Box 2.1). Such analysis shows that education policy in Switzerland is not efficient (Figure 2.2). Indeed, Germany and Switzerland had about the same score in the 2012 PISA reading assessment, but Switzerland spent 21.4% more per student than

Box 2.1. **Data Envelopment Analysis**

Data Envelopment Analysis (DEA) is a statistical technique used to assess the efficiency of public expenditure. Given that different combinations of inputs and outputs are observed in practice, DEA enables benchmarking of a country's performance against a set of best-practice countries by identifying how far it stands from the efficiency frontier. There can be a shortfall in terms of output, called output inefficiency, or an excess input, called input inefficiency. As a non-parametric technique, DEA does not require specifying a functional form for the implicit production function. The approach, however, is sensitive to sample selection and outliers. Sampling techniques such as bootstrapping can be used to correct for small-sample bias (Dutu and Sicari, 2015). Other OECD Surveys have used the technique, e.g. Slovenia (OECD, 2013e).

Figure 2.2. **Output inefficiency in secondary education,[1] 2012**

Potential gains in synthetic PISA scores, per cent[2]

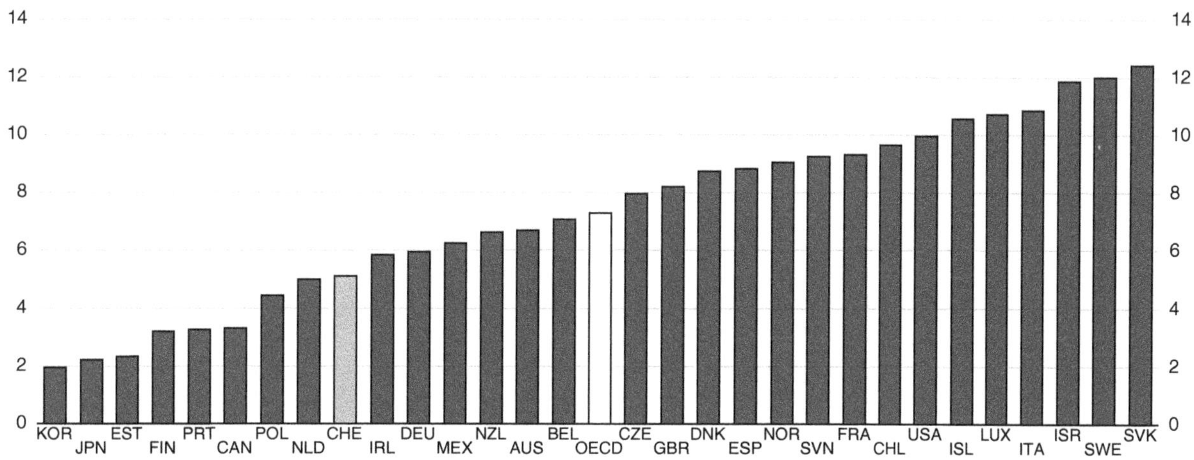

1. Data envelopment analysis (DEA) was performed with one output (PISA scores for 2012) and two inputs (a composite indicator of the socio-economic environment and lifestyle factors for the same year and PPP education spending). Averages over the periods 2009-11 were used for expenditure to capture its effects on performance and smooth its developments, as 2011 is the latest year available for education expenditure data.
2. Potential gains are measured if efficiency in a country were to be raised to the level implied by the estimated efficiency frontier while holding inputs constant and under the assumption of non-increasing returns to scale.

Source: OECD calculations.

StatLink http://dx.doi.org/10.1787/888933292647

Germany (see also Agasisti and Zoido, 2015). In health care, even though Switzerland is close to the frontier in terms of output efficiency, there remains much scope to improve input efficiency (Figure 2.3). For instance, in 2012 Switzerland had the largest health-care spending per capita in Europe at EUR 4 565 (adjusted for countries' different purchasing power), on par with Norway and well above the EU28 average of EUR 2 193 (OECD, 2014c). Note, however, that those figures include both public health-care expenditure (two thirds of the total) and private spending (the other third). Also worryingly, input efficiency has deteriorated for both education and health care since 2013 when similar DEA analysis by the OECD was last conducted (Hribernik and Kierzenkowski, 2013). Another example of poor efficiency, although this was not part of the DEA analysis, is Swiss agriculture. Despite heavy government support (direct payments are two thirds of farm income), it has the second-lowest productivity in the OECD (OECD, 2013b; Jarrett and Moeser, 2013).

Figure 2.3. **Output inefficiency in health care,[1] 2012**

Potential gains in health-adjusted life expectancy, per cent[2]

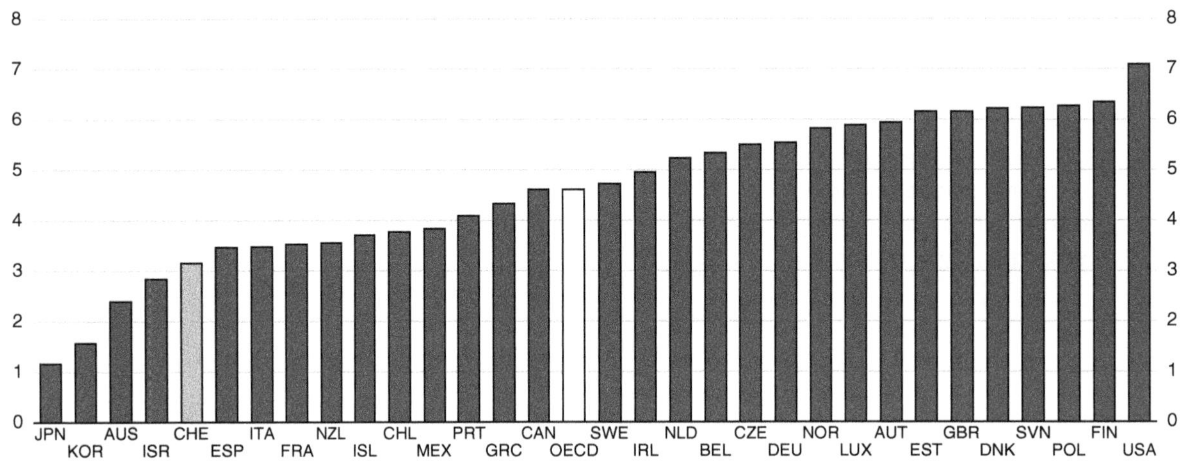

1. Data envelopment analysis (DEA) was performed with one output (health-adjusted life expectancy at birth for 2012) and two inputs (a composite indicator of the socio-economic environment and lifestyle factors for the same year and PPP health-care spending). Averages over the periods 2008-12 were used for expenditure to capture its effects on performance and smooth its developments.
2. Potential gains are measured if efficiency in a country were to be raised to the level implied by the estimated efficiency frontier while holding inputs constant and under the assumption of non-increasing returns to scale.

Source: OECD calculations.

StatLink http://dx.doi.org/10.1787/888933292653

By contrast, Swiss general public administration ranks first for output efficiency and third for input efficiency, with Switzerland improving on both dimensions since the previous DEA study (Hribernik and Kierzenkowski, 2013). For instance, Switzerland had the OECD's lowest ratio of administrative costs to net revenue collection in 2013 (OECD, 2015c). As noted earlier, it also has the lowest share of public employment, although many health-care workers are excluded. Perhaps as a result of the high performance by its public administration, Switzerland enjoys the highest public confidence in national government in the OECD (OECD, 2015c).

Efficiency in public spending is also about the optimal allocation of public funds. Indeed, the Swiss public sector operates under a set of institutional arrangements (fiscal equalisation across and within cantons, social security entitlements, debt-brake rules) that affect the allocation of public funds across levels of government and between areas of expenditure. For instance, because of spending constraints, the growing GDP share of pension entitlements may in the future crowd out other important expenditure categories, such as research or infrastructure.

This chapter is organised in two parts. First, production efficiency is examined in four of the main areas of public expenditure: education, health, transportation and agriculture. Several policy recommendations are made to maintain or increase output while reducing the costs and inputs needed. The second part of the chapter focuses on allocative efficiency of public spending. In particular, it examines to what extent social security funding, fiscal equalisation and public procurement can be improved in order to foster an efficient allocation of public funds across levels of governments and areas of public expenditure.

Increasing production efficiency

Making the education system more inclusive and responsive

Raising enrolment in early childhood education and care, especially for migrant children

Raising enrolment in early childhood education and care is one avenue to increase efficiency in the education system. In the OECD's PISA assessments, pupils are asked about the length of time they attended pre-primary education. Young people who stated that they had attended for more than a year achieved significantly higher values in the 2009 PISA reading tests in almost all countries compared to those who did not attend kindergarten at all (OECD, 2014a). Across OECD countries, enrolment of children at age three in pre-primary education has increased from 64% on average in 2005 to 70% in 2012 (OECD, 2015a). But in Switzerland, despite recent progress, childcare places are still in short supply, and only 3% of children aged three are enrolled in pre-primary education, the lowest rate in the OECD (Figure 2.4). And, indeed, participation in Swiss early-childhood education has declined since 2005, unlike almost all other OECD countries.

Figure 2.4. **Enrolment rates in early childhood and primary education at the age of three**

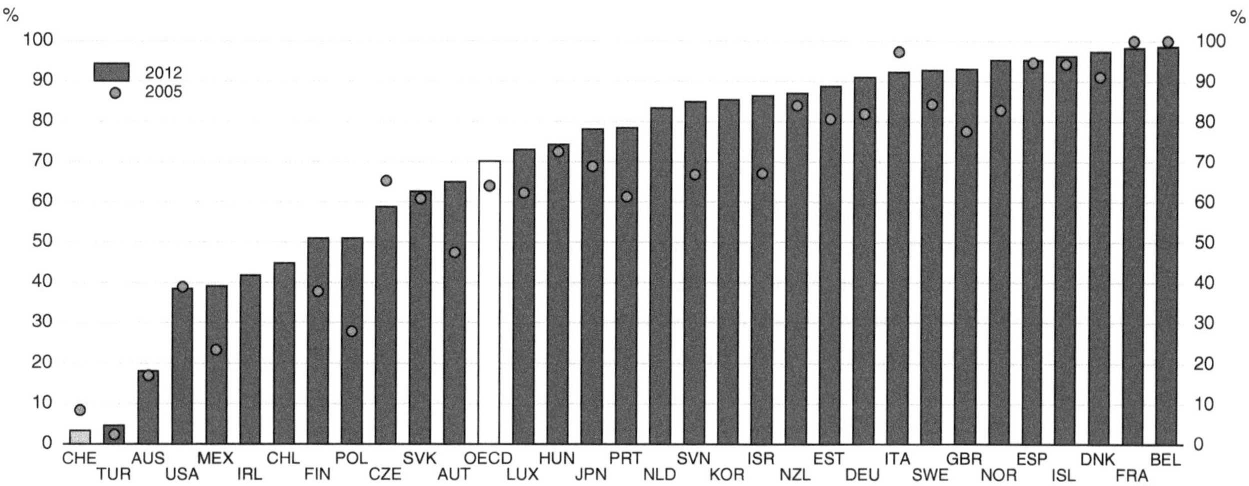

Source: OECD, Education at a Glance 2014 Database.

StatLink http://dx.doi.org/10.1787/888933292661

In order to alleviate the shortfall of childcare places, the Confederation launched a financial aid programme for childcare outside the family in 2003. This was initially to run for a period of eight years but has now been extended until 2019. In the programme's first 11 years, a total of 43 000 new places were created (*Le Temps*, 2014). Innovative initiatives such as the childcare voucher systems in the Canton of Lucerne have also been running successfully now, with a doubling of places since its 2009 inception. It is the lack of low-cost places that is especially problematic (OECD, 2013b). Region-based modelling of childcare costs shows, for instance, that Zurich has one of the most expensive childcare systems in the OECD for working couples once all costs are taken into account. Given the high marginal income tax on second earners, almost the entire second wage of an average dual-earner couple with two children aged two and three is needed to cover the cost of childcare (OECD, 2011). Similar conclusions were reached for canton Basel-Stadt (Schwegler et al., 2012). The government (cantons and municipalities) should increase direct public spending on additional pre-primary facilities, and the Confederation should institutionalise financial aid for childcare. Given the positive impact of pre-primary education on PISA scores and the positive relationship from such scores to economic performance (OECD, 2010c), the returns to such reforms are likely to be high.

Increased education spending on migrant children also promises above-average returns. In 2006 the Swiss Confederation and the cantons set an objective that 95% of all 25 year-olds hold an upper-secondary qualification. In the past 20 years that rate has fluctuated between 90 and 92% (CSRE, 2014). Looking closer, it turns out that the goal has now been reached for the Swiss born, but outcomes are still far from the target for those born abroad (Wolter, 2014). Some progress has been made, however. The PISA reading performance differential between young people with and without an immigrant background fell from 86 to 48 points between 2000 and 2009 (OECD, 2010a). In mathematics it fell from 76 to 63 points between 2003 and 2012 (OECD, 2014g). But roughly three-quarters of the narrowing, which primarily concerned first-generation migrants (i.e. young people who were not born in Switzerland), can be ascribed to an increase in immigration from countries such as France and Germany, whose languages overlap with Switzerland's (Cattaneo and Wolter, 2012).

The problem of underperforming native-born children of immigrants, already noted in the 2009 *Survey* (OECD, 2009), starts early. A survey of parents conducted in Basel and its environs showed that children with a migration background have the least opportunity to access facilities provided outside the family, thereby hampering their ability to master an official language early (CSRE, 2014). OECD research suggests that, despite improvements, immigration remains a risk factor for low academic performance which may have long-lasting consequences for individuals as they leave school and enter post-secondary education, training or the labour market (OECD 2012; OECD, 2015d). At the same time, empirical evidence shows that almost three quarters of the immigrant children's performance at school is accounted for by socio-economic determinants (Cattaneo and Wolter, 2015). This is supported by recent research which suggests that Switzerland performs relatively well regarding educational achievements of second-generation immigrants (Kunz, 2014). Switzerland should therefore boost assistance aimed directly at socio-economically disadvantaged families. It should also facilitate enrolment of children from families with an immigrant background in early childhood education and care.

Moreover, completing university has been shown to increase the earnings of Swiss men with disadvantaged family backgrounds even more than that of those from more favoured backgrounds (Perini, 2013). The outcome in terms of raising employment rates is lower, however (OECD and EC, 2015). If increased pre-primary spending helps to increase the probability that these children get to university level, the net return would be even higher. Overall, labour market outcomes for Swiss children of immigrants are highly favourable in international comparison. This is partly attributable to good overall labour market conditions and other factors such as the strong role of apprenticeship, which seems to be a particularly beneficial school-to-work transition mechanism for such children (Liebig et al., 2012).

Another contributing factor to weaker performance by children with an immigrant background is the lack of diversity among teachers. A quarter of the Swiss population was born outside of the country, but foreign-born students represent only about 8% of those planning to teach in compulsory education. A lack of linguistic and cultural diversity among the teaching profession can be problematic, in Switzerland as in other OECD countries, and a higher share of teachers from migrant families would help the integration of students from similar backgrounds. Specific measures such as those being implemented in Germany by the MigraMENTOR project could fruitfully be developed in Switzerland, making a teaching career more attractive to foreign students in particular (Box 2.2).

Box 2.2. **MigraMENTOR**

In some parts of Hamburg the share of children with an immigrant background is more than 30%, but teachers with the same background are less than 5%. The German Ministry of Education, together with several foundations, is trying to change this by attracting more migrant youths into teaching. Using their experience, teachers with a migrant background know what it means to grow up as a migrant, what the difficulties are, but also the opportunities. They are in a better position to motivate students, help them find their way through the German education system and show them that it is possible to be successful. Similar initiatives are now taking place in North Rhine-Westphalia and Berlin, where Humboldt University is touring secondary schools to promote teaching careers among migrant students.

Source: D. Bader and R. Fibbi (2012), *Les enfants de migrants: un véritable potentiel*, Étude réalisée sur mandat de la Commission Éducation et Migration de la Conférence suisse des directeurs de l'instruction publique (CDIP), Université de Neuchâtel.

The problem of inter-cantonal differences in standards

The number of student graduating high school with baccalaureate credentials in Switzerland has been increasing steadily, from 25% of the 1999 age cohort to around 36% nowadays. About 75% of that increase is due to an increase of holders of professional baccalaureates (CSRE, 2014). Whereas in cantons with a low baccalaureate graduation rate fewer than 10% of pupils fail to achieve competence level 4 in both reading and maths prior to entering a baccalaureate school, the figure in cantons with high baccalaureate attainment rates is about 30% (CSRE, 2014). In addition, the two cantons with the highest attainment rates also have the most pupils dropping out baccalaureate schools without the qualification.

That percentage is 50% in Geneva and a little over 40% in Ticino, both about triple the national average, whereas in Aargau virtually all pupils who begin complete the baccalaureate (Figure 2.5). In the end, students coming from cantons with high success rates score lower on competency tests and drop out more frequently from both baccalaureate schools.

Figure 2.5. **Premature exit from baccalaureate schools by canton**

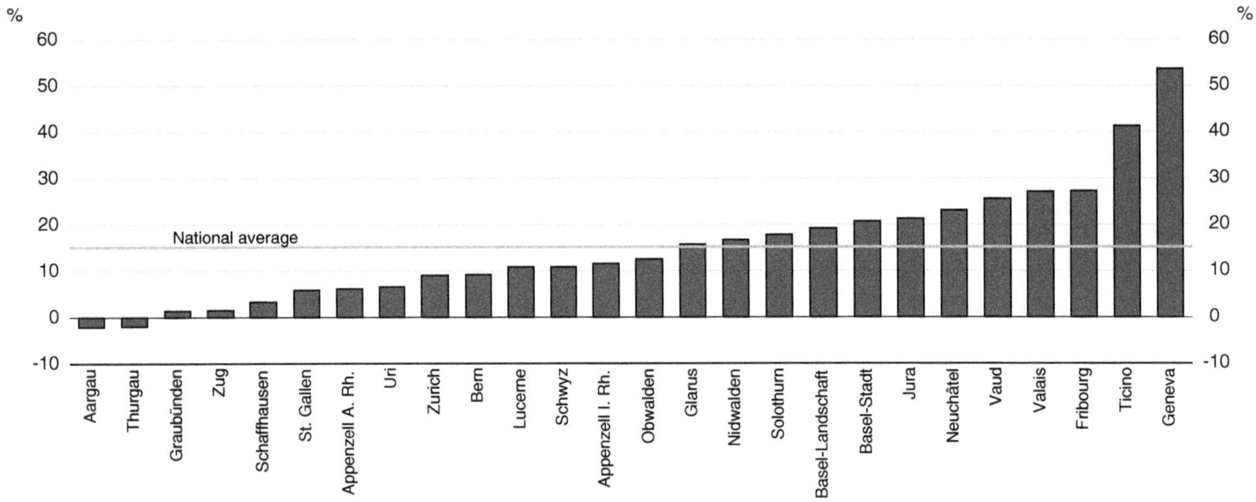

Source: CSRE, *Swiss Education Report* 2014, based on FSO data.

StatLink http://dx.doi.org/10.1787/888933292675

In Switzerland, with a few exceptions such as degrees in medicine, everyone who graduates from high school with a baccalaureate credential must be admitted to tertiary (type-A) education. However, baccalaureate graduates from certain cantons are overrepresented in university dropouts across Switzerland, suggesting that the quality of their baccalaureates is lower. The impact of the baccalaureate rate (expressed as the number of baccalaureates obtained as a percentage of the number of 19 year-olds) in the canton of origin has indeed been shown to increase the risk of dropping out significantly (Wolter et al., 2014). In addition to being unfair and inefficient, this imposes additional costs on the other cantons, which finance conventional universities, and the Confederation, which funds federal institutes of technology (e.g. ETH Zurich). One way to address this problem is to set up a bonus system to encourage such cantons to reduce the number of university dropouts, and vice versa. Indeed, education transfers already represent 60% of all inter-cantonal transfers (FFA, 2014b). The alternative of restricting entrance to universities via exams or other methods, would openly conflict with the affirmed objective to "maintain examination-free access to Swiss universities for baccalaureate holders", as agreed between the Confederation and the cantons (DFE, 2011). Another option would be to increase resources for guidance counselling for high school students, in particular with regard to field-of-study choices. In all instances, improving tracking and selection in cantons with high dropout rates should help contain the rise in university dropouts. Combined with a bonus-penalty, system it would help to raise Switzerland's DEA input efficiency in education. In addition, the dropout rates are particularly high among some foreign students. Therefore, solutions to reduce the dropout rate in the university system will have to be evaluated in a comprehensive way.

Problems in matching education with labour-market needs

While thousands of students drop out from academic baccalaureates and universities, the share of unfilled apprenticeships rose from 4% in 2007 to 9% in 2014. This represents 8 000 positions (8% of all apprenticeships) (LINK Institute, 2014). The main reason for unfilled places was the lack of suitable applicants; indeed, there was also a jump in firms saying they failed to receive any applicants for apprenticeships vacancies at all.

The increasing number of unfilled apprenticeships points to structural changes in the Swiss labour market, both on the supply and demand side. On the supply side, as discussed above, more students are enrolling in the academic track, and therefore fewer are enrolling in the vocational track where apprenticeship is a key component. On the demand side, despite the increasing number of unfilled apprenticeships, the percentage of firms offering such training has fallen, from 23% in 1985 to around 18% in 2008. In their analysis of Swiss companies' readiness to offer apprenticeships, Müller and Schweri (2012) find that the decline can be partly explained by the increasing proportion of very small businesses and start-ups. These firms typically offer fewer apprenticeships: newly established firms have a training rate of only 6.5% during the first four years, while the corresponding share of companies in existence for more than four years reaches 23.8%. Those trends can be problematic because the efficiency of the Swiss labour market relies heavily on the key role played by vocational education and training (VET) and professional education and training (PET) where apprenticeships are key (Box 2.3). Incidentally, VET graduates report the most satisfaction following their compulsory schooling, regardless of follow-on options (CSRE, 2014).

Box 2.3. **Vocational education and training**

In Switzerland more than 65% of students in upper secondary education are enrolled in pre-vocational or vocational programmes at the upper secondary level, compared with an average of only 44% across OECD countries. Among those who choose vocational programmes, about 93% of them are enrolled in joint vocational programmes combining school- and work-based elements. The VET system is well developed, and PET is well articulated with upper secondary VET, offering a wide range of progression opportunities.

Governments spent almost CHF 3 billion on VET in 2011. The cantons cover the majority of this funding, although from 2004 onwards, the Confederation increased its share from an initial 16% to the current 25% for VET/PET. About 10% of these Confederation funds is accounted for by expenditure on third-party projects, while the remaining 90% is paid as subsidies to the cantons. In 2009 more than CHF 5.3 billion was spent by companies on VET, with CHF 2.5 billion on apprentices' wages and the rest on investment. At the same time companies profit economically from offering apprenticeships (Strupler and Wolter, 2012).

Source: OECD (2014), *Education at a Glance 2014* – Country note for Switzerland, OECD Publishing; CSRE (Centre suisse de coordination pour la recherche en éducation) (2014), *Swiss Education Report 2014*, Aarau.

The demand for graduates in science and engineering, health care, teaching and in certain crafts is rising (B.S.S., 2014). This has contributed to a skilled labour shortage in those areas, which has been partly addressed by immigration, particularly from EU and EFTA countries. However, the passage of the "mass immigration" initiative in 2014 puts this strategy into question. The labour shortage in some areas such as STEM should be addressed by better selecting and matching students with labour market needs, and increasing the supply and attractiveness of fields of study that face high demand on the labour market.

Another inefficiency in the Swiss education system is overskilling among certain types of graduates. In 2011, about 30% of employed university of applied sciences (UAS) graduates were in a job that did not require a university degree (Figure 2.7), even five years after graduation. One explanation may be that some positions can equally be filled by people who have completed tertiary level B PET or those with continuing education and training certificates, a more professionalised form of tertiary education. A good example is the field of health: one year after graduation in the French-speaking part of Switzerland, where tertiary-level health training is only available at (type A) UAS, more than three-quarters of UAS graduates have found an appropriate job. By contrast, in German-speaking Switzerland, where nurses are also trained at tertiary level B, the rate is only one third (CSRE, 2014). Perhaps due to greater competition from VET and PET graduates, the share of UAS graduates with a master's degree who reported a good match between their training and their job one year after graduation in 2013 was lower than for conventional universities

Figure 2.6. **Match between job requirements and training one year after graduation from a UAS, 2011**[1]

Per cent

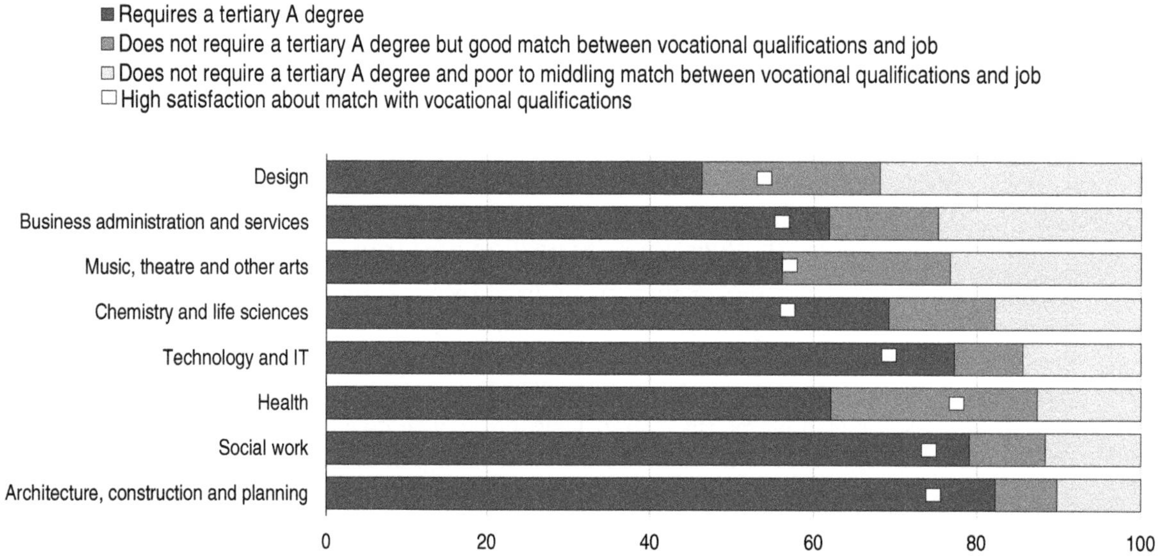

1. First-cycle graduates (Bachelor's degree) who had not enrolled for a Master's course at the time of the survey and second-cycle graduates (Master's).

Source: Swiss Education Report 2014, based on FSO data from the Graduate Survey.

StatLink http://dx.doi.org/10.1787/888933292680

Recommendations for promoting efficiency in education spending

- Increase public spending on early childhood education and care, especially for children with disadvantaged socio-economic backgrounds (including those from immigrant families), which could be combined with a generalisation of the childcare voucher systems in the Canton of Lucerne.
- Boost the number of teachers from immigrant backgrounds.
- Evaluate solutions to reduce the dropout rate in the university system.
- Boost the supply and attractiveness of fields of study that are in high demand in the labour market. Further clarify study streams across the tertiary education system.

(72.4% versus 84.4%). The government should look closely at the supply mix between general education type-A graduates and high-level technical type-B apprenticeships in the same field. The government should further clarify and differentiate study streams across the tertiary education system. Tertiary-type A and B education should be complementary, not substitutes.

Fostering value-based competition and better governance in health care

The Swiss health-care system is among the OECD's best. Patients benefit from high-quality services and from a wide choice of providers and insurers. This good performance is reflected in high levels of patient satisfaction: 19 years after the *Loi fédérale sur l'assurance-maladie* (LAMal), which introduced compulsory medical insurance, 94% of the Swiss are satisfied with the health care system, the highest level in the OECD (OECD, 2015c). But this excellence comes at a price. In 2012 Switzerland was on a par with Norway in terms of health-care spending per capita at EUR 4 565 (adjusted for countries' different purchasing power), more than double the EU28 average of EUR 2 193 (OECD, 2014c). With 68.4 persons employed in the health and social sector per 1 000 population, the overall supply of health personnel exceeds the OECD average. Most notably, Switzerland is above the OECD average for nursing, with 10.2 professional nurses per 1 000 population (OECD: 6.9) and 4.8 associate professional nurses per 1 000 population (OECD: 2.3).

Between 1996 and 2012 real health-care expenditure increased by 62%, and the average premium on a standard health plan for adults over 26 (adjusted for inflation) increased by 97% (Interpharma, 2015). In contrast, real GDP rose by 38% over the same period. Structural and demographic changes generate direct health-related costs that explain part of this rise. Population aging leads to higher medical expenses such as for long-term care, which, in addition, is less and less provided within the family. Long-term care has been the fastest growing component of health-care expenditure since 2000 (Figure 2.7). Some of the rising costs might be indirect through the increased political weight of the elderly population who support more public health-care spending (Zweifel et al., 2005). Some of the increase is also due to a "Baumol effect" (Baumol, 1961), whereby services in the health-care sector, especially in long-term care, are relatively more labour intensive and do not benefit from the same rate of productivity growth as the overall economy. But wages, which are an important cost-push factor in health care, grow at roughly the same rate as in other sectors, increasing the relative productivity-adjusted cost of the health-care sector. The idea has found some confirmation in empirical analyses (Hartwig, 2008).

Some of those inefficiencies are due to excessive fragmentation of the health system, leading to higher costs. It is the cantons that formally have the task of guaranteeing access to medical services and monitoring the system. They also take care of disease prevention and health education. The Confederation is responsible mostly for the regulation of health insurance. As for municipalities they handle the tasks that are delegated by cantons, for example the provision of nursing and home care. Fragmentation is also apparent on the funding side. In 2012, 61.3% of funds were provided by households, 32.3% by the government (Confederation 5.7%, cantons 22.3% and municipalities 4.3%) and 6.4% by private companies. By funding regimes, 42% came from the compulsory public insurance scheme (LAMal), 26.2% from households through a myriad of private health-insurance companies and out-of-pocket payments, 20.2% from the government (of which 17.1% from

Figure 2.7. **Decomposition of health expenditure developments and projections**

2000 = 100, per cent of GDP

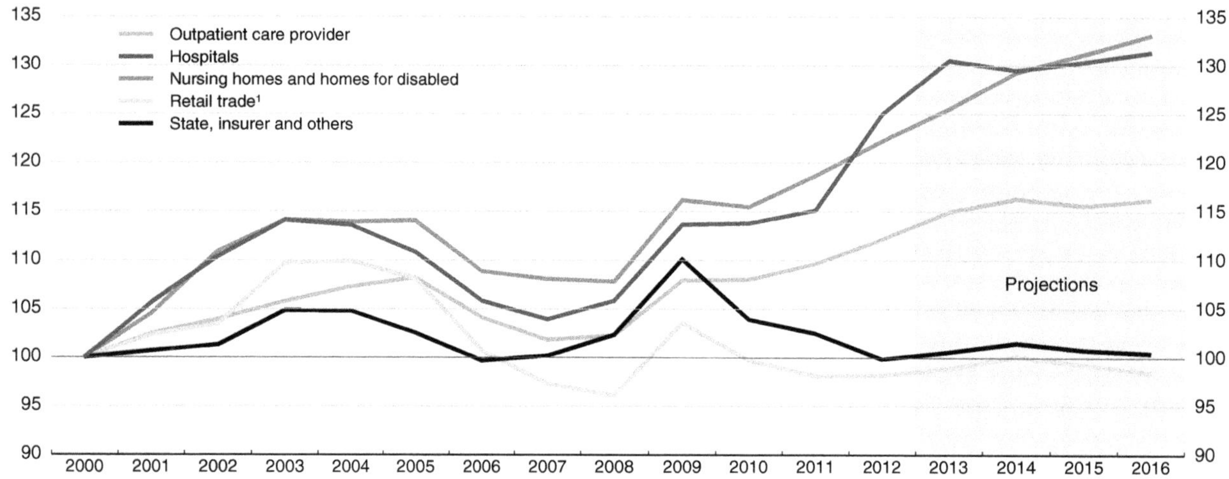

1. Pharmacies and all other possible selling points (supermarkets, stores, etc.).

Source: Federal Statistical Office (BFS); Federal Health Office (BAG); and KOF.

StatLink http://dx.doi.org/10.1787/888933292694

the cantons), 7.1% from private insurance and 4.5% from various other sources. Hospitals, clinics, birth centres and specialised institutions received 54.8% of the funds, the ambulatory sector 30.3%, retailers such as pharmacies 8.2%, and the rest (including non-profit institutions) 6.7% (BFS, 2014). One way to deal with the costs of fragmentation would be a single-payer public health insurance system, which would lead to greater transparency, accountability and economies of scale, but this was massively rejected by popular initiative ("Pour une caisse publique d'assurance-maladie") in September 2014. As a result, improvements will have to be made to the system as it currently operates.

One way to improve input efficiency is by encouraging competition to reduce costs for any given level of output. Consolidation in the sector has led to a fall in the number of health-insurance companies in the last 20 years, boosting economies of scale. The most sizeable consolidation has taken place in the smallest category (with less than 5 000 insured), with their number falling from 90 to 14 between 1996 and 2012 (Figure 2.8). However, incentives to compete on efficiency and the quality of healthcare services are blunted. First, the prices of services are often collectively negotiated at cantonal level between associations of insurers and providers. Moreover, Article 35 of LAMal obliges insurers to have contracts with all providers in a canton (the goal being to guarantee a diversity of approaches) regardless of costs and quality of service. Only formal proof of qualification and requirements with regards to infrastructure are needed to be admitted in the list of qualified providers, with no reference made to quality or cost efficiency. This prevents insurers from choosing providers on the basis of quality of care and makes it difficult to limit the number of providers and costs. At the same time, patients have little information on the quality of providers' services, and even if such information were available insurers could not benefit from it since they have to contract with all providers. Abolishing this obligation, while maintaining diversity, would increase efficiency by allowing insurers to pick the best, most cost-effective providers. It would also foster the development of a market for health-quality data in parallel to those collected by the cantons and the Confederation (see below).

Figure 2.8. **Number of insurers by size of their portfolio of insured people**

Insurance companies authorised to provide medical insurance

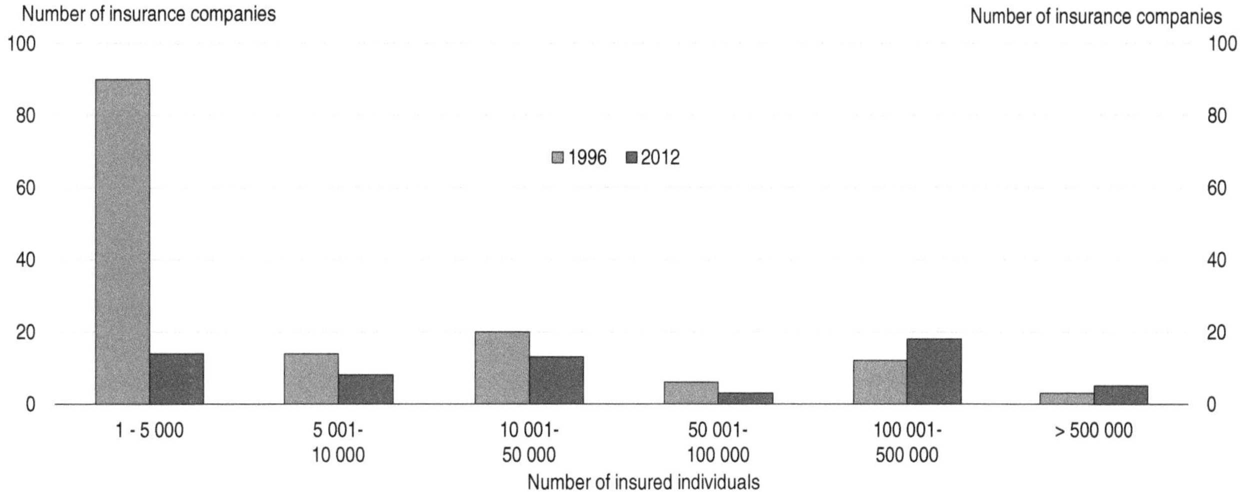

Source: Interpharma (2015), *Santé Publique en Suisse*, Basel.

StatLink http://dx.doi.org/10.1787/888933292700

Even greater efficiencies could be achieved by inducing a greater number of the insured to seek care within a restricted network of providers in exchange for lower health premiums, a system known as managed care. In addition to avoiding the costs of over-consultation, the system allows information sharing among practitioners within the network and facilitates quality certification. A comprehensive managed care system operates in a number of OECD countries, including the United States. Indeed, managed care is gaining in popularity in Switzerland, with 24% of insured people part of a managed care network in 2014, twice the 2010 share (Groupe Mutuel, 2015). Over-consultation can also be mitigated outside of managed care by "gatekeeping", i.e. requiring patients to be referred by generalists in order to access specialists or non-emergency hospital care.

One downside of managed care is that by offering premium discounts in exchange for restricting provider choice, managed care contracts are known to attract people with good health-risk profiles. As a result, higher-risk individuals are reluctant to switch to managed-care contracts, making it difficult to disentangle the impact of managed care from risk-selection. In order to foster real and equitable competition between insurers, further improvement in the current risk-equalisation mechanism would help. The mechanism organises risk-premium transfer payments through a risk-equalisation pool, but the formula currently corrects only for sex and age. Hospitalisation beyond three days in the previous year is now taken into account. More factors would be needed, some of which are currently being examined. While studies of the impact of managed care on cost savings controlling for risk-selection are scarce, they point to significant savings (OECD and WHO, 2011).

A by-product of the fragmentation of the Swiss health-care system is an over-supply of health services through "supplier-induced demand". Looking across cantons, there is a significant correlation between specialist density and the number of consultations (SAAS, 2012). No such correlation is evident for non-specialists, however, but Filippini et al. (2006 and 2009) have shown that a higher density of physicians is associated with higher antibiotic consumption, the annual cost of which is estimated at EUR 6.8 million, representing 12% of total spending on antibiotics in ambulatory care. Similar studies have shown that more beds lead to a greater use of hospital services. A side effect of this over-supply is that small hospitals tend to conduct too few operations to be cost effective, making it harder for them to keep up to date with quality standards. For instance, there are 120 hospitals conducting vascular surgery in Switzerland, versus 8 in the whole of London (*La Tribune de Genève*, 2015). Although the number of hospital beds per person in Switzerland is around the OECD average, there are many small regional hospitals with few beds. A reduction in their number should be encouraged. As with the other recommendations already discussed, it would raise Switzerland's input efficiency in health.

While consumers may choose between multiple providers, they often have surprisingly little quality information to inform their choices. As for health professionals, they lack registries publishing the results of specialised, complex treatments, which could be used as tools for comparative evaluation of the effectiveness and costs of treatments and health services. With an incomplete picture of how costly and effective treatments are and how health risks vary across the population, it is difficult for the insured to choose among providers and for governments to tailor policy. The resulting asymmetry of information generates over-consumption of medical services through supplier-induced demand, whose annual costs have been estimated at CHF 1-2 billion (SAAS, 2012).

Reflecting the organisation of the health-care system, health data are collected in a fragmented way. Quality data collection and diffusion lie in the hands of the Confederation, but the actual production and collection of underlying data rest with the cantons. As both owners and quality assurers of hospitals, cantons may have mixed incentives to address quality shortfalls. This is perhaps particularly a risk if the viability of local services is under threat. To make health policy evidence-based and tailor it to local circumstances, Switzerland would benefit from systematic collection of a set of data across the full spectrum of health services. Besides the quality indicators published by the Federal Office of Public Health, an organisation called the *Association nationale pour le développement de la qualité dans les hôpitaux et les cliniques* (ANQ) is now responsible for co-ordinating and producing quality indicators at hospitals and clinics around the country. Jointly funded by the cantons, the hospital association, Santésuisse (the umbrella organisation of health insurers) and several social insurance schemes, the ANQ programme has sought to measure a series of quality indicators. This includes rehospitalisation rates, surgical site infection rates, falls, ulcers and patient satisfaction (OECD and WHO, 2011). While participation is voluntary, the ANQ reports good will from most hospitals (ANQ, 2013). Nowadays uniform quality measures are computed for acute somatic illness, psychiatry and rehabilitation medicine. A set of quality indicators for primary care and outpatient activity is still lacking, however, and should be developed. In parallel, publishing a list of complying health-care providers could encourage voluntary participation.

The remuneration system for inpatient services provides another example of weak incentives to control costs. Hospitals used to receive funding based on the number of hospital beds occupied, inducing them to keep patients longer than necessary. A new system of case-based payments by diagnostic-related groups (DRGs) was introduced in January 2012. As in the US system, the payment per case is calculated by multiplying the base rate, which is hospital-specific, by a coefficient, which is disease-specific yet uniform at the national level. The coefficient reflects the relative costliness of hospital treatment for that particular condition. Base rates are negotiated between hospitals and insurers within each canton and approved by cantonal governments. The cost of in-patient drugs is included in the tariff, as are those of diagnostic and therapeutic services. Early evaluations show that costs are still rising fast (Table 2.1). While it is arguably too early to make a definitive assessment of the effects of the reform, it seems to be encouraging other inefficient behaviour such as providers selecting a costly DRG when the diagnosis is uncertain (Gerritsen and Kirchgässner, 2013). Moreover, the variation in hospital-specific prices (the base rates) remains high too. For instance, administrative tribunals validated base rates of CHF 10325 per case in Lucerne and CHF 9 480 per case in Zurich's Triemli and Waid hospitals. Those rates are significantly higher than the recommended base rate of CHF 8 974 derived from benchmarking of nationally efficient hospitals in the cantons of Zurich and Thurgovie (Confédération Suisse, 2014). The DRG reform is therefore a step in the right direction, but it has not removed all perverse incentives and has introduced others, and it leaves too much room for cantons to fix base rates. As noted earlier, more and better information via registries would help benchmark costs per procedure. If these measures and rulings by administrative tribunals prove insufficient, then new regulation may be needed to limit the ability of hospitals and insurers to set base rates.

Table 2.1. **Acute-care sector statistics in Switzerland**

	2011	2012	2013[1]
Number of hospitals	300	298	293
Number of hospital beds	38 533	38 297	37 744
Available hospital bed days (millions)	14.1	14.0	13.8
Number of days of hospitalisation (millions)	12.8	12.6	12.7
Occupancy rate (%)	91	90	92
Average length of stay (days)	9.5	9.4	9.4
Number of hospitalisations (millions)	1.35	1.35	1.37
Operating costs (CHF)			
Per case	11 631	12 251	12 564
Per day	1 229	1 320	1 357

1. Provisional.
Source: Interpharma (2015), *based on FSO data.*

With the long-term shift from treating communicable disease and accidents (curative care) to treating chronic conditions, the balance of effort in developed nations' health-care systems will need to shift from a far-reaching network of well-equipped hospitals to promoting good health throughout life via a focus on public health, prevention and primary care. The decentralised system has encouraged the development of locally relevant prevention programmes, but it has also made it difficult to develop broad-based policies to address major chronic diseases and conditions, such as diabetes, obesity and cancer, and associated risk factors (e.g. alcohol abuse). In addition, many of the 26 cantons are simply too small to achieve the minimum size for efficient prevention policy (the five least populated all have fewer than 40 000 inhabitants). Similarly, progress in implementing measures with a proven value has been too slow. An evaluation of Switzerland's H1N1 immunisation strategy found that cantons' response plans were not standardised nor harmonised to minimum standards, that there was a lack of co-ordination on the distribution of vaccines to cantons and that there was a lack of leadership in communication (OECD and WHO, 2011). The revision of the Epidemics Act, which will come into force in January 2016, creates a framework for up-to-date detection, monitoring, prevention and management of disease outbreaks. It requires, for instance, a co-ordinated approach to the development of emergency plans.

Drugs accounted for 9.2% of health costs and 20% of compulsory health-insurance expenses in 2012. Prices for medicines in Switzerland are much higher than in the comparison countries used for benchmarking by the Swiss Federal Office of Public Health (FOPH), namely Germany, Austria, Denmark, France, the United Kingdom and the Netherlands. Patented drugs for cardiovascular disease, for instance, are 11% cheaper in the FOPH panel countries, and 15% cheaper if Belgium, Finland and Sweden are included in an extended panel as the FOPH is currently considering. Generic drugs are on average 65% cheaper in the current comparison panel than they are in Switzerland. Their higher cost is due to the Swiss rule for setting their prices. The rule requires that generics be priced, depending on sales volume, at least 10% to 60% below the price of the original patented medicine at the time of its patent expiry. In addition, health insurance reimburses both the generic and the patented drug, thereby decreasing the incentive to choose the generic. As a result, the share of generics by value is low in international comparison (Figure 2.9).

Figure 2.9. **Share of generics in the total pharmaceutical market, 2013 (or nearest year)**

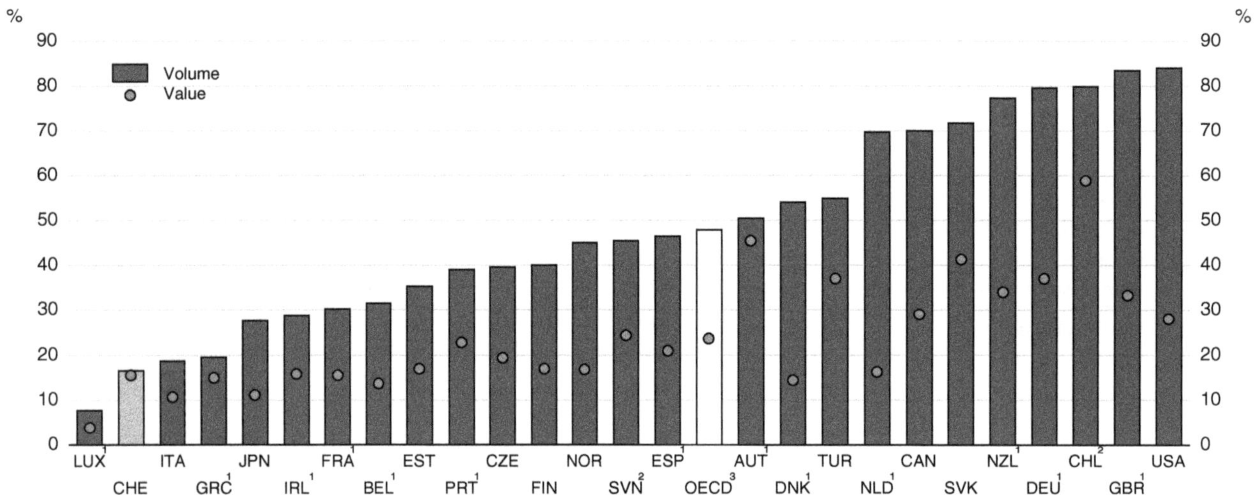

1. Reimbursed pharmaceutical market.
2. Community pharmacy market.
3. Simple average of the 26 countries with available data.

Source: OECD, *Health at a Glance 2015*.

StatLink http://dx.doi.org/10.1787/888933292422

Some progress has been made in reining in drug costs and boosting the use of generics, such as increasing the share paid by consumers for brand-name drugs for which less expensive generics are available (OECD and WHO, 2011). Perhaps as a result, drug spending fell below 10% of total health-care outlays in 2012 for the first time since LAMal in 1996 (Interpharma, 2015). Drug prices should be reviewed at least every year rather than every three years in order to better reflect varying exchange rates. In the autumn of 2014 prices of one-third of drugs were still using a 1.58 CHF/EUR exchange rate as a reference. Applying today's exchange rate of 1.04 CHF/EUR would therefore force prices down significantly. In any case, the current system for setting generics' prices should be abandoned in favour of reimbursing a pre-determined fixed amount, as is done in more than 20 other European countries (Confédération Suisse, 2014). Competition among pharmaceutical companies would push the price down to that level, and patients would have more incentives to choose the generic over the original. Such measures could save CHF 1 billion per year out of the CHF 5.7 billion spent on medicines, according to Santésuisse. This represents CHF 125 per patient per year.

The impact on health-care costs of allowing doctors to sell medicines is much debated. Using physician-level data for the period 2008-10, and exploiting regional variation in dispensing regimes across cantons, Kaiser and Schmid (2013) show that dispensing physicians (40% of the total) increase drug costs per patient by 30%. However, several other studies have shown that self-dispensing doctors have a mitigating cost-saving effect by prescribing generics more frequently where their profit margins are higher (Rischatsch et al., 2009). A study by Schleiniger et al. (2007) even found a robust negative effect of allowing doctors to dispense drugs on the volume of drugs sold.

Setting priorities in the Swiss health-care system is the shared responsibility of the federal government, the cantons and – in the field of care for older people – the municipalities. While the strongly local and participative nature of civic governance in Switzerland fosters locally relevant public health solutions, mirroring the situation discussed early regarding education, this dispersion in policy hinders the building of an overall vision for the health system and creates incentives that are not always geared towards efficiency. At some CHF 3 billion per year, inadequate co-ordination due to poor governance has been estimated by the Swiss Academies of Arts and Sciences to be the largest of all the system's inefficiency costs (SAS, 2012). Since many services are simultaneously financed from multiple sources, and nobody is responsible for the global health-care budget, it is easier for a financing body to cut its own outlays than to engage in more rational spending. As an example, if after an operation a patient is admitted to a nursing home, the overall costs will be higher than with at-home rehabilitation. But the proportion paid out by the health insurer for a nursing home assignment is much lower, so they prefer to send patients to nursing homes, increasing the overall cost (SAMS, 2012). This possibility to cost shift at the expense of another payer lowers incentives to look for solutions that would foster effective expenditure rationalisation. Such problems do not arise in countries with single payers (e.g. Scandinavia). Establishing a legal framework to facilitate national public health policies should then be a priority, as already highlighted in earlier OECD and WHO Reviews (OECD and WHO, 2006 and 2011). Such a law should clearly spell out objectives and priorities to ensure that cantons and insurers meet agreed outcomes. A national health conference gathering all stakeholders could be instituted to set priorities. A body in charge of implementing public health priorities and monitoring progress should also be put in place.

Recommendations for promoting efficiency in health-care expenditure

- Switch the system for setting generic drug prices to reimbursing a pre-determined fixed amount.
- Encourage systematic benchmarking of hospital costs. If hospital reimbursement rates keep rising despite the 2012 reform, consider new legislation to control them using cost benchmarks.
- Create incentives for agents to join managed-care networks, and further improve the risk-equalisation mechanism among insurers by including more dimensions in the formula.
- Encourage the closing of small and inefficient hospitals.
- Publish the list of institutions participating in the collection of quality data by the *Association nationale pour le développement et la qualité dans les hôpitaux et les cliniques* (ANQ), and develop quality indicators for primary care and outpatient activity.
- Establish a country-wide legal framework to set priorities and facilitate national public health policies.

Optimising the use of transport infrastructure

Between 2008 and 2013 the Swiss population grew by 5.8%, the seventh fastest in the OECD and the third fastest in Europe. Combined with a thriving economy and widespread commuting, this demographic growth is putting increasing pressure on the country's transport infrastructure. Using data from the Federal Roads Office, (FEDRO, 2013), OECD calculations point to the cost of traffic congestion reaching CHF 1 billion in 2013, three times as much as in 2000. In 2011, public spending on transport amounted to CHF 17.5 billion, 9% of total public expenditure (FSO, 2014). The financing of road and rail infrastructure, as well as of transportation services, relies on a combination of usage-based payments and public financing. Due to environmental concerns and Switzerland's peculiar topography (more than 70% of its area is covered by the Alps), extending existing infrastructure is difficult. Additionally, the estimated growth effect (beyond the capital expenditure) from additional rail tracks and motorway investment in Switzerland between 1960 and 2005 was weak, sometimes negative, pointing to poor-quality investment at the time (Égert et al., 2009).

More efficient use of transport infrastructure would over the long term reduce the need to invest in more of it. A particular feature of road and rail infrastructure usage is that congestion typically occurs in the morning and evening rush hours, as seen in passenger traffic data at Zurich's main train station for instance (Figure 2.10). Because road and rail infrastructure are "club" goods (i.e. excludable), their efficient use calls for congestion externalities to be internalised by charging a higher price at peak traffic times and vice versa ("peak-load pricing"). But road usage is largely free of charge in Switzerland. Motorway passenger vehicle users have to buy an annual CHF 40 vignette, while freight traffic is priced according to the distance travelled. Neither pricing scheme is time-dependent, however.

Figure 2.10. **Hourly distribution of train passengers, Zurich Hauptbahnhof, 2014**[1]

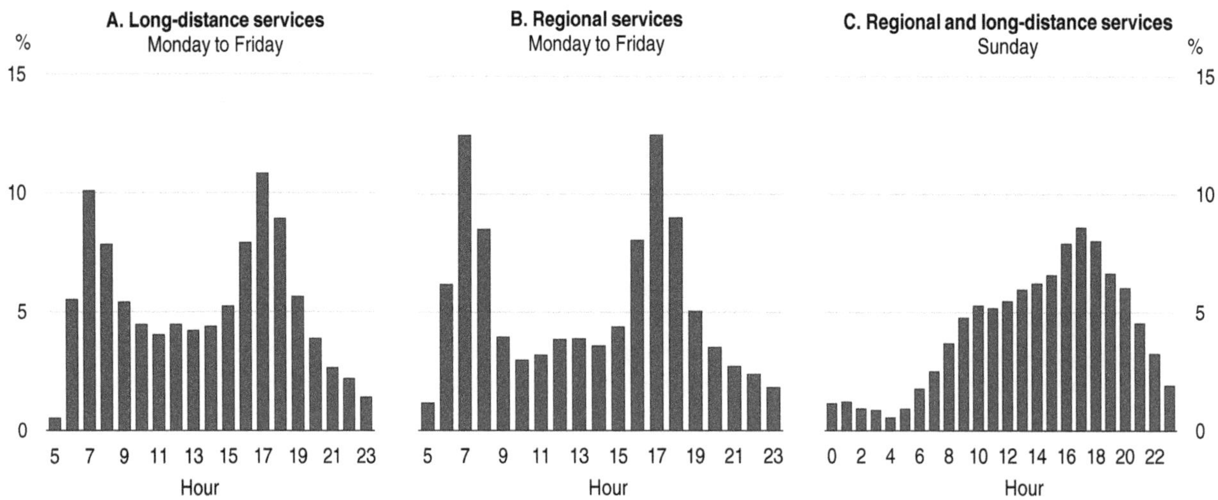

1. Passenger traffic as a percentage of trains arriving at or departing from Zurich HB per hour. On weekdays the percentage per hour before 5 A.M. is negligible.

Source: SBB, Die SBB in Zahlen und Fakten 2014, Bern.

StatLink http://dx.doi.org/10.1787/888933292718

Peak-load pricing for train travel would be easy to implement. Recent technological advances such as electronic tolling stations or satellite-based registration systems also make it possible to charge for road usage according to time. A mileage rate could be charged for all vehicles, with tariffs differentiated by time, place and possibly type. However, this may cause transparency problems (with drivers not knowing what they were being charged) and privacy issues. Moreover, because usage-dependent pricing for only one mode of transportation might lead to a substitution effect, it is important to adopt a comprehensive pricing framework (Avenir Suisse, 2013a). If congestion pricing encourages travel on other congested routes, the result can be sizeable indirect welfare losses, which counteract the intended efficiency gain (Parry and Bento, 2002). Peak-load pricing might also raise efficiency beyond the gains due to more uniform traffic by reducing the need for additional infrastructure and therefore taxes to fund it. This so-called double dividend is well-known in environmental economics where green levies yield a first dividend by internalising environmental externalities and a second by allowing lower distortionary taxes (Bovenberg and De Mooij, 1994). Switzerland should implement peak-load pricing, as already long ago advocated by the OECD (Blöchliger, 2002). It should first test the system on a few heavily used highways, such as between Bern and Zurich or between Geneva and Lausanne. As illustrated by the Dutch experience, rapid implementation is critical. Party politics and the fall of the government on another issue put an end to the idea, despite strong initial support from all sides of the Dutch society (ITS-CH, 2013; OECD, 2010b). Addressing the privacy issue is also important.

Recommendation for promoting efficiency in transport

- Test peak-load pricing on some highly trafficked roads. Further build peak-load pricing into rail fares.

Enhancing competitiveness and efficiency in agriculture

At 0.7% of GDP versus 2% in the median OECD country, agriculture plays a relatively minor role in the Swiss economy. Its share in employment is larger, at 4.1%, reflecting low productivity (Figure 2.11, Panel A). Indeed, the Swiss farming sector is made up of relatively small family farms, and many agricultural policies support extensive farming practices. Consolidation of the sector is ongoing, however, with the number of farms declining from 70 537 to 56 575 between 2000 and 2012 and the average farm area increasing from 15.2 to 18.3 hectares. Agricultural land, including alpine pastures (which accounts for 36% of total land), shrank by 5.4% between 1985 and 2009 as a result of increases in urban and wooded areas. Livestock and crops represent 69% and 31% of total agricultural production by value, and milk is the primary output (OECD, 2014d).

Swiss agriculture has long been heavily shielded from market forces. For instance, in the 1980s, domestic food prices were on average 4.5 times higher than world prices. A set of policy reforms implemented in the early 1990s substantially reduced market distortions. In particular, a larger share of support is now delivered through less distortive direct payments, rather than market price support (Box 2.4). As a result, domestic prices moved closer to world market levels, and OECD Producer Support Estimates (PSEs) for Switzerland fell from 78% in 1986-88 to 53% in 2011-13. Nevertheless, prices paid to producers were still around 40% above the world market level in 2013 (before the latest franc appreciation), and PSEs remain among the highest in the OECD (Figure 2.11, Panel B). Such high levels of support result in considerable costs for taxpayers. In 2013, total budgetary outlays amounted to CHF 3.7 billion, which represented 5.8% of total federal budgetary

Figure 2.11. **Low productivity and high support in agriculture**

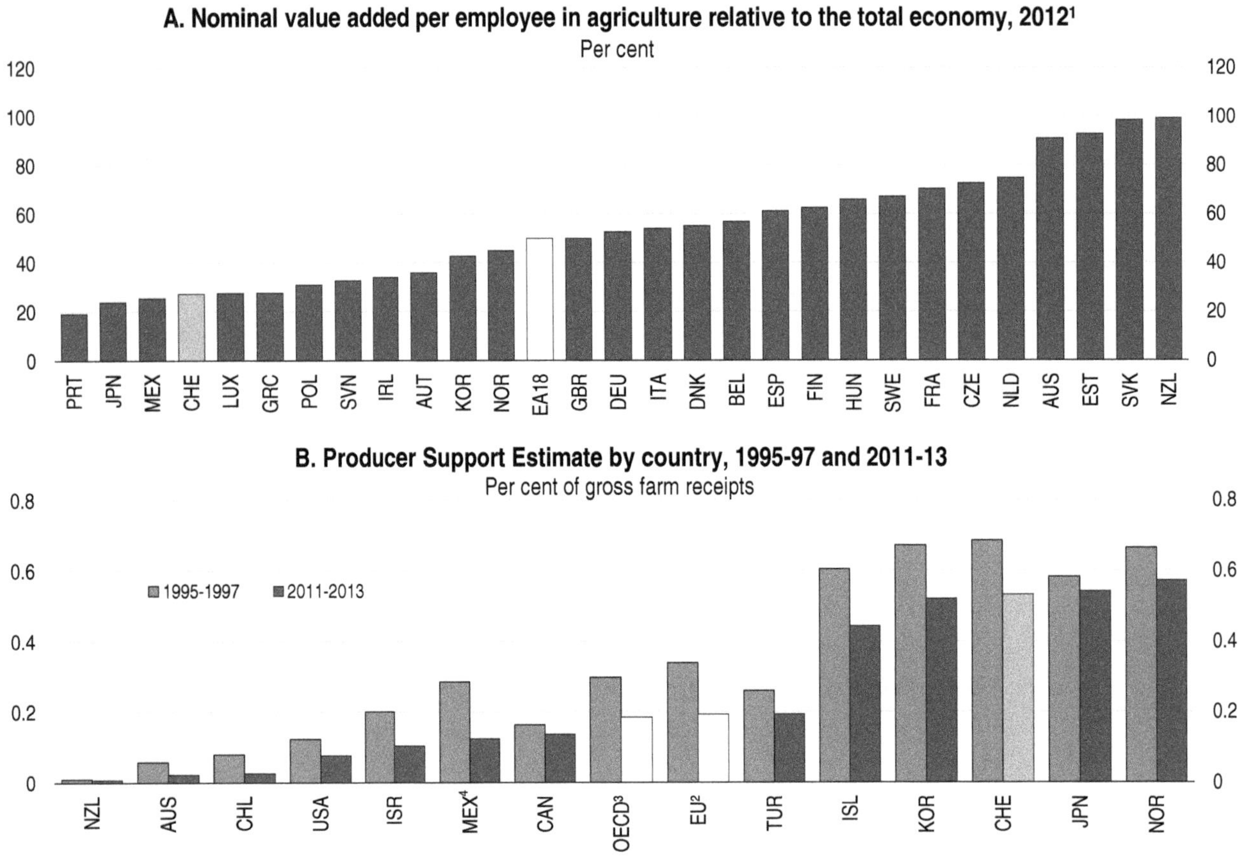

1. Or latest year available.
2. EU15 for 1995-97 and EU27 for 2011-13.
3. The OECD total does not include the non-OECD EU member states.
4. For Mexico, 1991-93 instead of 1995-97.

Source: OECD *National Accounts* and *Agriculture Statistics Databases.*

StatLink http://dx.doi.org/10.1787/888933292727

expenditures (0.6% of GDP) (FOAG, 2014). Total support, as measured by the Total Support Estimate (TSE), amounts to just over 1% of GDP, 58% of which is paid for by taxpayers and 42% by consumers (Jarrett and Möser, 2013).

The pace of reform in the agricultural sector has slowed in recent years, and barriers to structural changes remain significant (OECD, 2013b). While the shift toward direct payments (which are less distortive than price support) has improved efficiency, they still represent nearly two-thirds of Swiss agricultural GDP, leaving little room for what farmers earn by selling their products on the market. As a result, price signals are playing only a secondary role in guiding farming decisions. This is likely to hamper the development of a competitive food-producing sector that responds efficiently to evolving consumer preferences (OECD, 2015b). Future policy changes should aim at reducing the overall level of agricultural support, inducing farmers to produce more efficiently. Similar in spirit to ecological direct payments, some of the general direct payments could be transformed into efficiency direct payments, that is, payments conditional on implementing productivity-enhancing farming methods. Similarly, some of the general direct payments could be made conditional on increasing the share of revenues coming from market activities.

Box 2.4. Direct payments in Swiss agriculture

A new system of direct payments was gradually introduced starting from 1993. There are two main categories of direct payments. General direct payments are non-commodity-specific payments granted in the form of payments per hectare of farmland, per head of cattle, for roughage-consuming cattle and for farming in difficult locations. They represented CHF 2 147 million in 2013, more than half of which absorbed by area payments. The other type are ecological direct payments, which are granted in the form of area and headage payments to farmers who voluntarily apply stricter farming practices than those required by public regulations and fulfil the criteria of proof of ecological performance. They aim at achieving environmental and animal welfare targets. In 2013 they represented CHF 645 million, the main category being "regularly keeping animals outdoors" (CHF 166 million).

Switzerland adopted a new policy framework for the period 2014-17 (Politique Agricole 2014-17). The main change is the suppression of general area payments and the reallocation of payments more closely related to specific objectives (agricultural practices) complemented by a system of transition payments to make the reform socially acceptable. Another important shift is the replacement of general headage payments to ruminants by an area payment to pastures with a requirement for a minimal stocking density. Most of the animal welfare and agri-environmental payments from the previous period continue to be applied under this new framework. The environmental cross-compliance conditions are also maintained in the new system of payments. The overall annual budgeted amount for these payments remains stable for the whole period at around CHF 2.8 billion (USD 3.0 billion), which is around the same level as in 2012 and 2013.

Source: OECD, *Review of Agricultural Policies: Switzerland 2015.*

Barriers to trade also weigh on efficiency in agriculture and should be reduced further. Tariff protection varies substantially across and within sectors, averaging 32% for agricultural products versus 1.4% in Australia and 9% in the United States, with adverse effects on productivity (WTO, 2013, 2014 and 2015). Agro-food imports are also regulated by a complex system of tariff-rate quotas. The system takes nearly 300 pages to describe; it has 28 tariff quotas, 58 sub-quotas and 80 bilateral preferential tariff quotas other than those under the Generalised System of Preferences where all imports are admitted freely (OECD, 2015b). The elimination of the remaining export subsidies to processed products (exporters of processed foods are compensated for the high costs of locally produced inputs) should also be considered to further reduce interference with domestic and world markets.

Agricultural spending also suffers from distortions arising from inconsistencies between policy instruments and objectives. For example, payments to maintain cattle production in geographically less favoured areas create incentives to increase stocking densities on grassland (pastures). This, in turn, increases environmental pressures from livestock farming, which conflicts with the environmental objectives supported by ecological direct payments (OECD, 2015b). Similarly, high tariffs on agricultural products raise the price of imported raw materials used in the food processing industry, which hampers the ability of domestic food producers to sell competitively priced items. As for general direct payments, they slow down the necessary structural changes in the farming sector by maintaining production where it is not economically viable and by restricting expansion in the more productive lowland regions. The latest *OECD Review of Swiss Agricultural Policies* (OECD, 2015b) calls for more explicit disentangling of policy objectives and instruments via a differentiated policy approach. In particular, it recommends distinguishing between policies that address market failures and those that address farmers' income problems.

Recommendations for promoting efficiency in agriculture

- Using environmental direct payments as a model, allocate some of the general direct payments to create: 1) "efficiency" direct payments conditional on implementing productivity-enhancing farming methods; and 2) 'market' direct payments to farmers who increase the share of their revenue coming from market-related activities rather than direct payments.
- Reduce import tariffs on agricultural products and export subsidies to processed food producers.
- Disentangle agricultural policy objectives and instruments by distinguishing between policies that address market failures and those that address farmers' income problems.

Allocating public expenditure efficiently

With public debt at around 45% of GDP (or 35% of GDP according to Maastricht definition), down 10 percentage points since 1998, Switzerland's public finances are in very good shape. The cantons have declining debt-to-GDP ratios, thanks to good economic conditions and debt-limitation mechanisms. Indeed, "debt brake" rules, which were put in place in the 1990s for most cantons and in 2001 for the Confederation, have undoubtedly contributed to a decline in debt-to-GDP ratios (Figure 2.12). However, the picture is more mixed for municipalities and the social security system. In particular, the outlook for social

Figure 2.12. **Trends in the gross debt-to-GDP ratio by level of government, 1990-2014**[1]

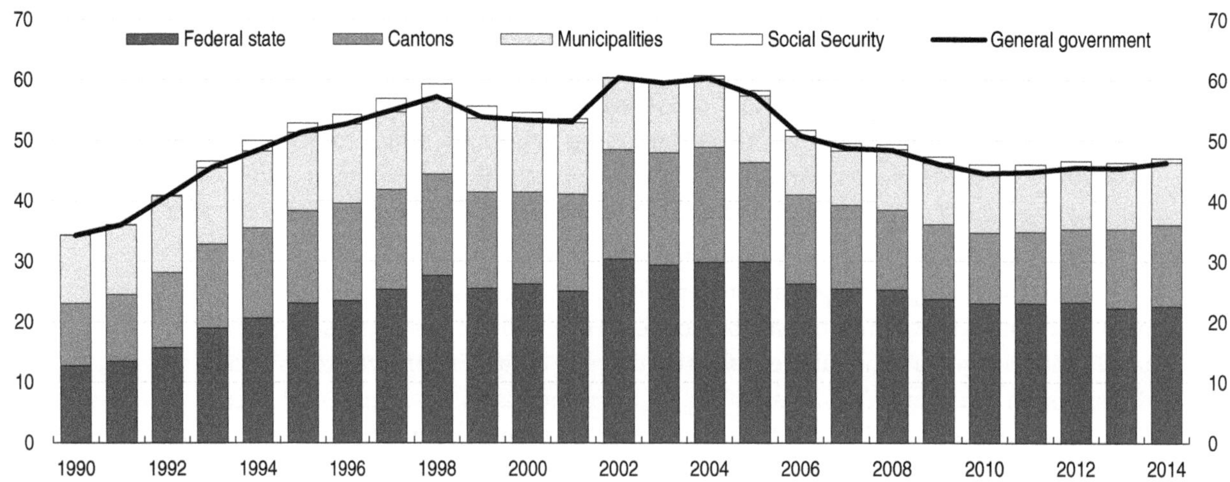

1. Data for 2014 are projections in the case of Cantons and Municipalities and, consequently, for the general government.
Source: Federal Finance Administration (FFA).

StatLink http://dx.doi.org/10.1787/888933292738

security spending is increasingly beholden to demographic forces and risks crowding out other categories of public spending. National and cantonal fiscal equalisation systems are also impacting on the allocation of public funds across levels of government and expenditure areas. This section looks at how those constitutional arrangements and obligations could be improved to foster an efficient allocation of public expenditure and to avoid the risk of important categories being underfunded. It also makes policy recommendations to increase the role and efficiency of tendering for public procurement as a cost-effective way to deliver high-quality public services.

Tackling the rise in pension expenditure

While keeping the debt of the Confederation and the cantons under control via debt-brake rules is effective, almost 40% of all public spending consists of social security expenditures (FFA, 2014a). Yet, with the exception of some relatively small federal transfer payments, social security expenses, such as the public old-age pension insurance, are excluded from federal accounts and therefore unconstrained by its debt brake. Also, importantly, many social insurance expenses are related to demographic factors, such as aging, which will put increasing pressure on public expenditures regardless of the strength of the economy. Projections show that if growth rates in social and health spending were to continue on their current trajectory, their share in total public spending would jump to 70% by 2030 (économiesuisse, 2012). The biggest increases will relate to the old-age pension system, whose cost is predicted to increase from 9.6% to 11% of GDP in 2030, and long-term care, from 0.6% to 1.9%. Further simulations that encompass all areas of public spending confirm that the biggest increase in public debt will relate to social security (Figure 2.13). If no corrective actions are taken, public debt could rise to over 130% of GDP by 2060 (FDF, 2012).

Figure 2.13. **Public finance projections**

Debt-to-GDP ratio, baseline scenario

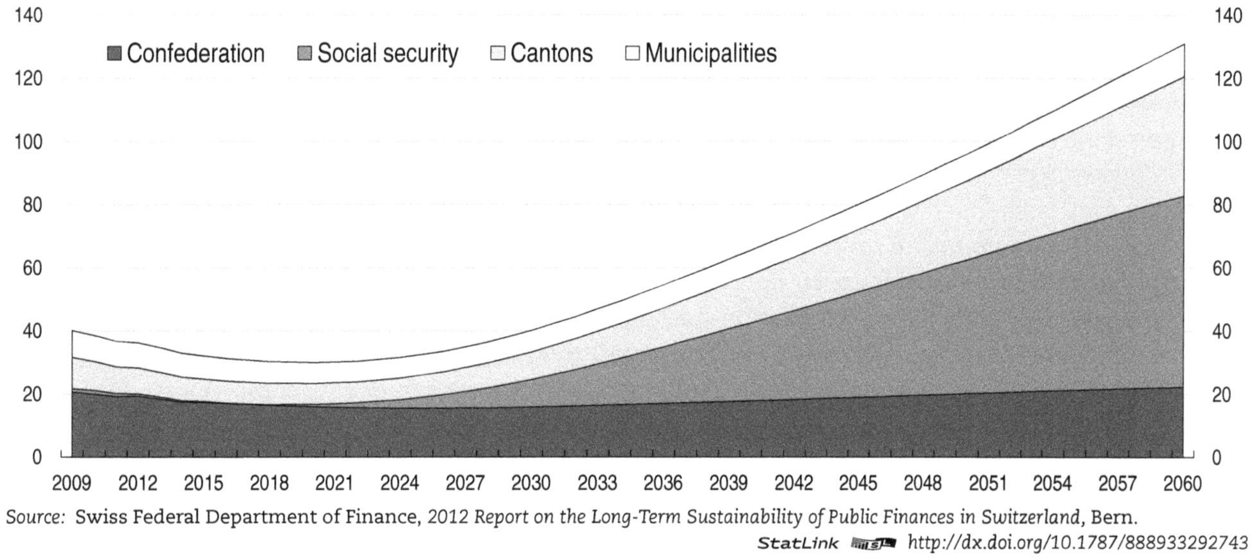

Source: Swiss Federal Department of Finance, *2012 Report on the Long-Term Sustainability of Public Finances in Switzerland*, Bern.

StatLink http://dx.doi.org/10.1787/888933292743

In the Swiss social insurance system, both entitlements and contributions are set by law with no guarantee that the latter will fully cover the former (Bruchez and Matter Schaffner, 2011). By leaving this key aspect of public finances to the side, the debt brake may be misleading by giving the impression that public finances will always be under control. While there is always the option to amend the debt brake, as was done in 2008 to incorporate extraordinary spending, debt brake rules are not the right tool to control social expenditure. Moreover, incorporating such spending would risk crowding out other important productivity-enhancing outlays on education and transport, for instance. There is already some crowding out going on via the old-age pension system, since about 20% of its expenses are covered by the Confederation, as are 38% of invalidity insurance (AI) outlays (Bruchez and Matter Schaffner, 2011).

The Swiss pension system has three pillars. The first is the public old-age pension system (AVS). It is a defined-benefit system and is largely financed out of labour income contributions. Since 1975 the contribution rate has been 8.4%, which is paid in equal proportions by employees and employers. The second largest source of financing is the federal budget, which covers about 20% of AVS expenses. The remainder, about 6%, comes from earmarked tax revenues, such as the tobacco tax. The formula behind entitlement payments uses the number of years in which contributions have been made and past annual incomes. The second pillar is a funded system. It is financed out of labour income contributions by employers and employees and the return earned on the accumulated stock of capital. The contribution rate increases with the employee's age, from 7% between 25 and 34 years old, to 18% between 55 and 64/65 years old. Employers are required to contribute by at least as much as the employee. The third pillar is a system of tax-deductible private saving, capped at CHF 6 768 per year for employees who are part of the second pillar. With rising life expectancy and declining fertility, the ensuing decline in the ratio of workers to retirees is going to be a challenge for the first pillar as pension spending is financed by contributions from current workers. From 6.2 workers per pensioner in 1950, the ratio fell to 3.8 in 2010 and is projected to drop to 2.0 by 2050 (Avenir Suisse, 2013b). At the same time the fertility rate has dropped from 2.7 to 1.5 since the mid-1960s.

All else being equal, the effects of aging on the financing of social security can be offset in three ways: by increasing revenues (higher contributions), decreasing expenses (reduced benefits) and raising the retirement age. Any reform needs to account for the impact that it would have on labour supply (which is the contribution base for social security), the total tax take and finally economic growth. A comprehensive, general equilibrium assessment taking into account all interactions was conducted by Keuschnigg et al. (2011). In their overlapping-generations model, they aimed at keeping benefits unchanged while varying contributions, the retirement age (currently 65 for men and 64 for women) and several key features of the Swiss system. In line with demographic projections, the authors assumed that the dependency ratio roughly doubles due to increased longevity, total population rises by 10% in the long run, and the working-age population declines by about 6%. Several reforms were considered in the modelling exercise, such as raising the retirement age, eliminating the upper income ceiling for pension assessment (currently contributions on income above CHF 79 560 do not translate into higher first-pillar pensions), eliminating unemployment benefits from the contribution base (which weakens job-search intensity), boosting competition among pension funds and reducing their administrative costs, and encouraging life-long training.

The modelling showed that if the government leaves current benefit rules unchanged and adjusts taxes and contribution rates to balance budgets, the statutory labour tax burden has to rise by 21 percentage points, total employment falls by 11.8% in absolute levels and GDP per capita falls by 20%. However, a large part of the negative consequences of ageing can be offset by a comprehensive reform package to boost aggregate labour supply and, thereby, the contribution base. The most effective measure by far was found to be by increasing the retirement age by four years, which keeps the system balanced without adjustments to contribution and pension replacement rates. Intuitively, longer lived future generations need to roughly split their extended total lifetime between work and retirement in the same way as present generations do. If agents currently spend three-quarters of their adult lives in work and one quarter in retirement, then each additional year of life expectancy should be divided in the same way. As for the VAT rise, because it taxes consumption rather than labour, it is found to be less harmful for labour supply than wage taxes, as it is also a tax on retiree wealth imposed when it is spent. Several OECD countries such as Iceland, Israel and Norway already have an official retirement age of 67. Switzerland should raise the retirement age to 65 for both sexes and thereafter link it to life expectancy.

As part of this concern to boost labour supply, especially in old age, any pension reform could be fruitfully augmented with appropriate flanking policies. Indeed, one way to increase the labour supply is to "work better with age" by optimising the possibilities for employment throughout people's lives (OECD, 2014e). In that regard Switzerland is doing well, with one of the highest employment rates for older workers in the OECD. In 2014, 71.6% of Swiss aged 55-64 were in work, behind Iceland (84.2%), New Zealand (76.2%), Sweden (74.2%) and Norway (72.2%), but easily exceeding the OECD average of 56%. That strong performance is mainly attributable to men with degrees under 60, however (Düll and Sonnet, 2014). At 20.3%, the employment rate for workers aged 65-69 places Switzerland 14th among the 34 OECD countries, far behind the best score of 48% for Iceland (OECD, 2014e). In line with previous *Survey* recommendations, one option to boost labour supply of older workers is to pay higher pensions to people who work beyond the normal retirement age. For instance, pensions are raised by 12% in Portugal for every year of additional work, 10.4% in the United Kingdom and 8.4% in Japan. In Switzerland pensions go up only between 5.2% and 6.3% (OECD, 2013a). Another option is to continue to reduce existing incentives for early retirement, especially in the second pillar, which range from mandatory early retirement to very attractive packages for the most successful employees. Also, on-the-job training for people aged 55-64 without a university degree is seven times lower than that for workers with a degree. Targeted programmes should be developed to raise the skills of older workers without degrees. In Switzerland, only 665 companies (slightly above 1%) employ staff who are beyond the legal retirement age (*Le Temps*, 2015). Thus in Switzerland, like in France, Norway and the Netherlands, more could be done on the demand side to encourage employers to hire and retain workers approaching and beyond retirement age (Sonnet et al., 2014). The Swiss government is moving in the right direction. It decided to have regular meetings with the social partners and the cantons to discuss best practices regarding the employability of older workers. The first meeting took place in April 2015.

A comprehensive pension reform (Prévoyance Vieillesse 2020) encompassing the first and second pillars is currently being discussed in Parliament. The main changes are a harmonisation of the retirement age between sexes (at 65 years, currently 65 for men and 64 for women), an increase in the VAT rate by 1.5 percentage points to fund the first pillar, more flexibility in the transition to retirement (allowing, in particular, for a gradual transition), and a decrease from 6.8% to 6% of the "conversion rate" in the second pillar (the annual pension as a share of cumulated retirement savings).

Recommendations for tackling the rise in pension expenditure

- Fix the retirement age at 65 for both sexes and thereafter link it to life expectancy.
- Pay a higher retirement premium for working beyond the retirement age, and reduce existing incentives for early retirement.
- Develop programmes to raise the skills of older workers without degrees to help them be productive longer.

Improving the efficiency of fiscal equalisation

The goal of fiscal equalisation is to provide minimum acceptable levels of public services across heterogeneous jurisdictions without requiring heavier tax burdens. Fiscal equalisation in Switzerland is implemented via a transfer of fiscal resources across jurisdictions with the aim of offsetting differences in revenue-raising capacity and public service costs (Blöchliger and Charbit, 2008). In Switzerland, National Fiscal Equalisation exists between the Confederation and the cantons, but each canton also has its own equalisation system for its municipalities. There are two main components to equalisation between the Confederation and the cantons: resource equalisation and cost compensation. There is also a cohesion fund worth CHF 366 million, which aims to cushion the effect of recent reforms and is intended to last until 2036.

Resource equalisation is based on the revenue potential of the cantons, which is determined by the taxable income and assets of individuals and the taxable profits of companies. Revenue potential is used to compute a normalised average, say 100, and then cantons are divided into the financially strong and weak (those with outcomes greater or lower than 100). Weak cantons receive transfers from the financially strong cantons (horizontal resource equalisation) and from the Confederation (vertical resource equalisation). An important part of the resource equalisation system is to allow poorer jurisdictions to compete tax-wise with fiscally stronger ones (Oates, 2003). Therefore, fiscal equalisation provides some levelling of the playing field in the competition for economic attractiveness.

Cost compensation addresses variations in costs across cantons associated with geographical, topographic and socio-demographic factors that result in differing requirements or costs of delivering public services. Typically, the alpine cantons have higher costs for infrastructure, winter road maintenance and schools (e.g. school buses), while urban cantons have an above-average proportion of poor and foreign residents who require more assistance. In 2014 resource equalisation amounted to CHF 2.2 billion from the Confederation to the cantons and CHF 1.5 billion among the cantons – that is CHF 3.7 billion in total. Cost compensation amounted to CHF 0.7 billion, half for topo-geographic factors and half for socio-demographic factors, all from the Confederation (Dafflon, 2014). The total of nearly CHF 4.5 billion represented 0.7% of GDP.

At the federal level, an important reform of fiscal equalisation and task allocation between the cantons and the Confederation was adopted by referendum in 2004. A recently published report concluded that implementing the reform has been successful on many fronts (Conseil Fédéral, 2014). For instance, the report noted that the share of non-earmarked transfers increased from 24% to 40%, in line with the goal of reinforcing autonomy. It also noted that the target level of financial resources per capita of 85% of the

Swiss average was exceeded in all cantons over the study period. The disentanglement of tasks and financing was also achieved, with 17 of a total of 33 formerly shared tasks disentangled. The Confederation is now solely responsible for seven task areas (including motorways, the old-age pension system and invalidity insurance) and the cantons for ten (including institutions for the disabled and schools for children with special needs). The Confederation and cantons continue to assume joint responsibility for 16 task areas (including regional traffic).

Several problems remain. The very nature of the transfer system creates the risk that the resources transferred to the cantons do not match their needs. For instance, there have been cases of overcompensated cantons with respect to the legal criterion of 85% of the national average of resources per capita (Taboga and Utz, 2014). Indeed, the effect of adjusting transfers cannot be known before the next periodic report on fiscal equalisation by the Federal Council due in 2018, which is also sub-optimal. By then it may well be that cantons will have been undercompensated or overcompensated again. It would be useful to understand the precise reasons for overcompensation and then to amend the transfer formula accordingly.

With regard to decreasing discrepancies in financial capacity and fiscal pressure, not much progress has been made since the 2004 reforms. Although several cantons have been able to lower their tax rates, this was mainly attributable to good economic conditions and the dividends paid by the Swiss National Bank to the cantons, rather than to National Fiscal Equalisation itself. However, the current system creates little incentive for less wealthy cantons to raise their resource potential: the equalisation framework operates so that cantons face a corresponding decrease in fiscal transfers, on average equal to 80% of the revenue raised (Conseil Fédéral, 2014). The implied implicit tax rate of 80% should be reduced to a more incentive-compatible rate, say 60%. In order to attract businesses while limiting the rise in revenue potential, a smaller weight should be put on companies' profits in the calculation of resource potential, as discussed in the draft corporate tax reform package. Furthermore, it would be worth investigating if moral hazard is a real issue. Other issues relate to the financial capacity of cantons to deal with changing cost structures. For instance, the current 50-50 allocation between socio-demographic factors and topographic/geographic factors in the cost equalisation scheme does not take into account the growing role played by socio-economic factors and is therefore detrimental to more urbanised cantons. The equalisation scheme should be amended to take into account the realities of modern Switzerland.

Recommendations for improving efficiency in fiscal equalisation

- Decrease the high implicit tax rate on cantons that increase their revenue potential to be no more than 60%, and lower the weight on companies' profit in the calculation of resource potential.
- Consider lowering transfers to cantons whose tax effort is below the average of the paying cantons
- Make efforts to better understand the causes of over- and under-compensation, and amend the transfer formula accordingly.

Increasing the share of public procurement put out to tenders

By outsourcing and tendering contracts, governments can deliver high-quality public services at lower cost. In Switzerland public procurement represented 25% of public spending in 2013, up from 23% in 2011, but below the OECD average of 29% and only half the maximum of 45% (in the Netherlands) (OECD, 2013b; OECD, 2015c). At 5.3%, expenditures on general government outsourcing as a percentage of GDP were also the second lowest in the OECD in 2013, less than a third of the share in the Netherlands.

Following signing in April 1994 the WTO-negotiated Agreement on Government Procurement, Switzerland liberalised its public procurement system to make it more transparent and equitable. This was facilitated by the December 1994 Federal Law on Public Procurement (and implementing ordinances) and the Intercantonal Agreement on Public Procurement, which together form the legal basis for public tenders in Switzerland (Oesch, 2010). Access to the market is further governed by the 1995 *Loi sur le marché intérieur* and several other regulations. In addition, Switzerland and the EU signed a bilateral agreement on public procurement in 1999. It is part of a package of seven sectoral bilateral agreements (*Package I*), which is now under threat following the passage of the 2014 mass immigration initiative. The agreement with the EU extends WTO treatment to procurement by municipalities, to private companies exercising public functions in the areas of water, electricity and gas, as well as to procurement by the state-owned telecoms and railway operators (Schneider et al., 2014). In addition to fostering efficiency gains by opening Swiss public tenders to European firms, the agreement with the EU also opened an EU procurement market worth an estimated CHF 1 500 billion per year to Swiss companies (économiesuisse, 2014).

Raising the share of public spending allocated via tendering and improving the existing framework could lower public expenditure. Despite the adoption of WTO principles, significant inefficiencies remain in the current tendering system due to lack of homogeneity in procedures across cantons and the Confederation. More harmonisation is required, especially since 80% of all tenders are advertised by sub-national governments (i.e. the cantons), one of the highest shares in the OECD (OECD, 2013d). In line with recommendations made in the 2007 *Survey*, progress was made with the modification of the implementing ordinance in 2008, which aimed at simplifying and accelerating procurement procedures as well as regulating the use of more transparent e-procurement (OECD, 2007 and 2009). A revision of legal frameworks is currently underway and includes an alignment of cantonal and federal legislation with the revised WTO General Procurement Agreement, which came into force in April 2014. This should lead to greater standardisation in procedures and foster fair and transparent competition. Switzerland should implement standardised procedures for all its jurisdictions.

As part of its effort to increase transparency, Switzerland should also track procurement spending more systematically in order to increase accountability in the procurement process and also to see who benefits the most. It has indeed been shown that, compared to their share in Swiss GDP, firms from French- and Italian-speaking cantons are under-represented in contracts awarded by the Confederation and its bodies. Language in particular is a problem, with some calls for tenders requiring submissions to be in German only (CGSO, 2014). Measures should be taken to effectively eliminate discriminatory practices, which are forbidden by the 1995 *Loi sur le marché intérieur*. Switzerland should also publicise plans for future procurement tenders, as is done in several other countries, as a way to help interested companies plan ahead (OECD, 2013d).

A web platform (*www.simap.ch*) was launched in March 2009 to centralise and harmonise the advertisement of tenders and data collection for applicants. In 2014 the amount of public contracts advertised via the website totalled CHF 13.1 billion, 20% of total public expenditure (Tanner, 2015). The OECD Council Recommendation on Public Procurement encourages the use of digital technologies to ensure transparency, foster competition and achieve greater value for money in public procurement. The Swiss *e*-Procurement platform only allows for the publication of tender notices. The *e*-Government programme identified the need to expand the website's functionalities to allow businesses to download information about public tenders and submit their bid electronically. In 2014, bidder profiles and standardised forms were introduced. The upload function should be integrated at a later point in time to enable users to submit bids electronically. Beyond these implemented or planned functionalities, the platform does not provide any capacities that relate to contract implementation and management (orders, e-invoicing, performance assessments).

Recommendations for using procurement to raise public spending efficiency

- Increase the share of public expenditure allocated via public tenders.
- Harmonise procurement procedures across jurisdictions. Raise transparency by systematically tracking and advertising procurement outcomes. Expand the functionalities of *www.simap.ch*.

Bibliography

Agasisti, T. and P. Zoido (2015), "The Efficiency of Secondary Schools in an International Perspective: Preliminary Results from PISA 2012", *OECD Education Working Papers*, No. 117, OECD Publishing.

ANQ (2013), *Rapport Annuel de l'ANQ*, Association nationale pour le développement de la qualité dans les hôpitaux et les cliniques, Bern.

Avenir Suisse (2013a), *Mobility Pricing: Wege zur Kostenwahrheit im Verkehr*, Zurich.

Avenir Suisse (2013b), *Une cure de jouvence pour la prévoyance vieillesse : Propositions de réforme du deuxième pilier*, Zurich.

Baumol, W.J. (1967), "Macroeconomics of unbalanced growth: The anatomy of urban crisis", *American Economic Review*, Vol. 57, pp. 415-26.

BFS (2014), *Statistiques de la Santé 2014*, Bureau of Federal Statistics, Neuchâtel.

Blöchliger, H. (2002), "Road- Pricing – eine alternative Route zur heutigen Strassenfinanzierung", Die Volkswirtschaft 5-2002, pp. 4-7.

Blöchliger, H. and C. Charbit (2008), "Fiscal Equalization", *OECD Economic Studies*, No. 44, 2008/1, pp. 1-22.

Bovenberg, A.L and R.A. de Mooij (1994), "Environmental levies and distortionary taxation", *American Economic Review*, Vol. 84, pp. 1085-89.

Bruchez, P.A. and E. Matter Schaffner (2011), "Des règles budgétaires pour les assurances sociales", *La Vie Économique*, 1/2-2011, pp. 27-30.

B,S,S. Volkswirtschaftliche Beratung AG (2014): *Fachkräftemangel in der Schweiz – Ein Indikatorensystem zur Beurteilung der Fachkräftenachfrage in verschiedenen Berufsfeldern*. Studie im Auftrag des Staatssekretariats für Wirtschaft (SECO), Basel.

Cattaneo, M. and S. Wolter (2012), "Migration policy can boost PISA results: Findings from a natural experiment", *IZA Discussion Paper Series*, No. 6300, pp. 1-19.

Cattaneo, M. and S. Wolter (2015), "Better Migrants: better PISA Results. Findings from a Natural Experiment", *IZA Journal of Migration*, forthcoming.

CGSO (2014), *Déséquilibre entre régions linguistiques lors de l'octroi des commandes de la Confédération et des régies fédérales: la CGSO et l'Office fédéral des constructions et de la logistique s'engagent pour corriger la situation*, Communiqué de presse, 26 novembre, Conférence des Gouvernements de Suisse Occidentale, Bern/Fribourg.

Confédération Suisse (2014), *Rapport annuel du surveillant des prix*, Bern.

Conseil Fédéral (2014), *Rapport sur l'évaluation de l'efficacité 2012-15 de la péréquation financière entre la Confédération et les cantons*, Bern.

CSRE (2014), *Swiss Education Report 2014*, Centre suisse de coordination pour la recherche en éducation, Aarau.

Dafflon, B. (2014), "Fiscal Equalization: The Swiss way, federal, cantonal, local", presentation at the *Fiscal Equalization Transfers – International Perspectives: Lessons for Poland* conference, 11-12 December, Warsaw.

DFE (2011), *Valorisation optimale des chances, Déclaration 2011 sur les objectifs politiques communs concernant l'espace suisse de la formation*, Département Fédéral de l'Économie, Bern.

Düll, N. and A. Sonnet (2014), "Continuer à travailler après 55 ans: la Suisse pourrait faire mieux ", *La vie économique*, 11-2014, pp. 49-52.

Dutu, R. and P. Sicari (2015), "An Application of Data Envelopment Analysis to Swiss Public Expenditure", *OECD Economics Department Working Paper* (forthcoming).

économiesuisse (2012), *Garantir la pérennité des assurances sociales grâce à des mécanismes d'intervention*, dossier politique, No. 19, Geneva.

économiesuisse (2014), *Comment la Suisse bénéficie des accords bilatéraux*, dossier de travail, pp. 1-6.

Égert, B., T. Koźluk and D. Sutherland (2009), "Infrastructure and Growth: Empirical Evidence", *OECD Economics Department Working Papers*, No. 685, OECD Publishing.

EUROSTAT (2015), *Mortality and life expectancy statistics*, Kirchberg, Luxembourg.

FDF (2012), *2012 Report on the Long-Term Sustainability of Public Finances in Switzerland*, Federal Department of Finance, Bern.

FEDRO (2013), *Trafic et disponibilité des routes nationales, Rapport annuel 2013*, Federal Roads Office, Bern.

FFA (2014a), *Les Finances Publiques 2014, Mémento Statistique*, Federal Finance Administration, Bern.

FFA (2014b), *Statistique financière 2012 de la Suisse, Rapport annuel*, Federal Finance Administration, Bern.

FOAG (2014), *Rapport Agricole 2014*, Federal Office for Agriculture, Bern.

FSO (2014), *Mobility and Transport, Pocket Statistics 2014*, Federal Statistical Office, Neuchâtel.

Filippini, M., G. Masiero and K. Moschetti (2006), "Socioeconomic determinants of regional differences in outpatient antibiotic consumption: Evidence from Switzerland", *Health Policy*, Vol. 75, Issue 1, pp. 77-92.

Filippini, M., G. Masiero and K. Moschetti (2009), "Small area variations and welfare loss in the use of outpatient antibiotics", *Health Economics, Policy and Law*, Vol. 4, Issue 1, pp. 55-77.

Gerritsen, B. and G. Kirchgässner (2013), "Le système de santé suisse", *La Vie Économique*, 5/2013.

Groupe Mutuel (2015), *Les réseaux de soins, qualité et couts au défi*, LOGIN, Martigny.

Hartwig, J. (2008), "What drives health care expenditures? – Baumol's model of unbalanced growth revisited", *Journal of Health Economics*, Vol. 27, pp. 603-23.

Hribernik, M. and R. Kierzenkowski (2013), "Assessing the Efficiency of Welfare Spending in Slovenia with Data Envelopment Analysis", *OECD Economics Department Working Papers*, No. 1058, OECD Publishing.

Interpharma (2015), *Santé Publique en Suisse*, Basel.

ITS-CH (2013), *Priority topic: Mobility Pricing: Traffic management or financing*, Report, 20 November, Intelligent Transport System – Switzerland, Basel.

Jarrett, P. and C. Moeser (2013), "The Agri-Food Situation and Policies in Switzerland", *OECD Economics Department Working Papers*, No. 1086, OECD Publishing.

Kaiser, B. and C. Schmid (2013), "Does Physician Dispensing Increase Drug Expenditures?", *Discussion Paper*, No. 13-03, University of Bern.

Keuschnigg, C., M. Keuschnigg and C. Jaag (2011), "Aging and the Financing of Social Security in Switzerland", *Swiss Journal of Economics and Statistics*, Vol. 147, No. 2, pp. 181-231.

Kunz, J. (2014). "Analyzing Educational Achievement Differences between Second-Generation Immigrants: Comparing Germany and German-Speaking Switzerland", *German Economic Review* (forthcoming).

La Tribune de Genève (2015), "Le réformateur des hôpitaux suisses était genevois", 29 May.

Le Temps (2014), "Les crèches peuvent respirer jusqu'en 2019", 17 September.

Le Temps (2015), "Avenir Suisse défend la flexibilité des retraites", 28 January.

Liebig, T., S. Kohls and K. Krause (2012), "The labour market integration of immigrants and their children in Switzerland", *OECD Social, Employment and Migration Working Papers* No. 128, Directorate for Employment, Labour and Social Affairs, OECD Publishing.

LINK Institute (2014), *Baromètre des places d'apprentissage*, Rapport détaillé, August.

Müller, B., and J. Schweri (2012), "Die Betriebe in der dualen Berufsbildung: Entwicklungen 1985 bis 2008", Bureau of Federal Statistics, Neuchâtel.

Oates, W.E. (2003), "Assignment of Responsibilities and Fiscal Federalism", in *Federalism in a Changing World, Learning From Each Other*, pp. 39-50, Blindenbacher and Koller (eds), Kingston-Montreal.

OECD and WHO (2006), *OECD Reviews of Health Systems: Switzerland*, OECD Publishing and WHO (Geneva).

OECD and WHO (2011), *OECD Reviews of Health Systems: Switzerland*, OECD Publishing and WHO (Geneva).

OECD (2007), *OECD Economic Survey of Switzerland 2007*, OECD Publishing.

OECD (2009), *OECD Economic Survey of Switzerland 2009*, OECD Publishing.

OECD (2010a), *PISA 2009 Results: Learning Trends. Changes in student performance since 2000*, Vol. V, OECD Publishing.

OECD (2010b), *OECD Economic Survey of the Netherlands 2010*, OECD Publishing.

OECD (2010c), *The High Cost of Low Educational Performance, The long-run economic impact of improving PISA outcomes*, OECD Publishing.

OECD (2011), *Doing Better for Families*, OECD Publishing.

OECD (2012), *Untapped Skills: Realizing the potential of immigrant students*, OECD Publishing.

OECD (2013a), *Pensions at a Glance 2013-OECD and G20 Indicators*, OECD Publishing.

OECD (2013b), *OECD Economic Survey of Switzerland 2013*, OECD Publishing.

OECD (2013c), *Government at a Glance 2013*, OECD Publishing.

OECD (2013d), *Implementing the OECD Principles for Integrity in Public Procurement, Progress since 2008*, OECD Public Governance Reviews, OECD Publishing.

OECD (2013e), *OECD Economic Survey of Slovenia 2013*, OECD Publishing.

OECD (2014a), *Does pre-primary education reach those who need it most?, PISA in Focus*, OECD Publishing.

OECD (2014b), *Education at a Glance – Highlights*, OECD Publishing.

OECD (2014c), *Health at a Glance, Europe 2014*, OECD Publishing.

OECD (2014d), *Agricultural Policy Monitoring and Evaluation 2014, OECD Countries*, OECD Publishing.

OECD (2014e), *Vieillissement et politiques de l'emploi, Suisse – Mieux travailler avec l'âge*, OECD Publishing.

OECD (2014f), *Education at a Glance – OECD indicators*, OECD Publishing.

OECD (2014g), *PISA 2012 Results: Excellence through Equity, Giving Every Student the Chance to Succeed*, Vol. II, OECD Publishing.

OECD (2015a), *Education Policy Outlook 2015, Making Reforms Happen*, OECD Publishing.

OECD (2015b), *OECD Review of Agricultural Policies: Switzerland 2015*, OECD Publishing.

OECD (2015c), *Government at a Glance 2015*, OECD Publishing.

OECD (2015d), "Can the performance gap between immigrant and non-immigrant students be closed?", *PISA in Focus*, Vol. 53.

OECD/European Union (2015), *Indicators of Immigrant Integration 2015: Settling In*, OECD Publishing.

Oesch, M. (2010), "Évolution du droit des marches publics en Suisse", *La Vie Économique*, Vol. 3, pp. 5-9.

Palumbo, G., G. Giupponi, L. Nunziata, and J. Mora-Sanguinetti (2013), "Judicial performance and its determinants: a cross-country perspective", *OECD Economic Policy Papers* No. 5, OECD Publishing.

Parry, I. and A. Bento (2002), "Estimating the welfare effect of congestion taxes: The critical importance of other distortions within the transport system", *Journal of Urban Economics*, Vol. 51, pp. 339-65.

Perini, L. (2012), "Peer effects and school design. An analysis of efficiency and equity", *IRENE Working Paper Nr. 12-01*, IRENE Institute of Economic Research, Neuchatel.

Rischatsch, M., M. Trottmann, and P. Zweifel (2009), "Do Physicians' Financial Interests Undermine Generic Substitution? A Study of Imperfect Agency", manuscript, University of Zurich, December.

SAAS (2012), Effizienz, Nutzung und Finanzierung des Gesundheitswesens, Swiss Academy of Arts and Sciences, Bern.

SAMS (2012), "Sustainable Medicine", position paper, Swiss Academy of Medical Sciences, Basel.

SBB (2014), *Die SBB in Zahlen und Fakten 2014*, Schweizerische Bundesbahnen, Bern.

Schaltegger, C.A., R. Hofmann and Z. Huwyler (2015), "La péréquation financière au banc de la pratique: l'exemple de Bâle-Campagne", *La Vie Économique*, 1/2-2015, pp. 41-45.

Schleiniger, R., T. Slembeck and J. Blöchliger (2007), "Bestimmung und Erklärung der kantonalen Mengenindizes der OKP-Leistungen", manuscript, ZHAW School of Management and Law, Winterthur.

Schneider, M. E., M. Scherer, B. Ehle and S. Moss (2014), *Construction in 31 jurisdictions worldwide 2015 (Switzerland)*, pp. 156-61, Lalive, Geneva/Zurich.

Schwegler, R., S. Stern and R. Iten, R. (2012), "Familienfreundliche Steuer- und Tarifsysteme. Vergleich der Kantone Basel-Stadt und Zurich", Schlussbericht, Infras, Zurich.

Sonnet A., H. Olsen and T. Manfredi (2014), "Towards More Inclusive Ageing and Employment Policies: The Lessons from France, the Netherlands, Norway and Switzerland", *De Economist*, Volume 162, December.

Strupler, M. and S. Wolter. (2012): *Die duale Lehre: eine Erfolgsgeschichte – auch für die Betriebe. Ergebnisse der dritten Kosten-Nutzen-Erhebung der Lehrlingsausbildung aus der Sicht der Betriebe*, Rüegger, Glarus, Chur.

Taboga, S. and P. Utz (2014), "Le deuxième rapport sur la péréquation financière: revue de détail d'un pilier du fédéralisme", *La Vie Économique*, 10/2014, pp. 38-41.

Tanner, M. (2015), "La plateforme pour les marchés publics Simap.ch s'est imposée", *La Vie Économique*, 7/2015, pp. 28-31.

Wolter, S. (2014) "Paysage éducatif suisse: les principaux chantiers sont toujours là", *La Vie Économique*, 1-2/2014, pp. 44-47.

Wolter, S., A. Diem and D. Messer (2014). "Drop-outs from Swiss Universities: an empirical analysis of data on all students between 1975 and 2008", *European Journal of Education*, Vol. 49, Issue 4, pp. 471-83.

WTO (2013), *Trade Policy Review, Review by the Secretariat: Switzerland and Liechtenstein*, WT/TPR/S/280, 19 March.

WTO (2014), *Trade Policy Review, Review by the Secretariat: The United States*, WT/TPR/S/307, 11 November.

WTO (2015), *Trade Policy Review, Review by the Secretariat: Australia*, WT/TPR/S/312, 3 March.

Zweifel, P., L. Steinmann and P. Eugster (2005), "The Sisyphus syndrome in health revisited", *International Journal of Health Care Economics and Financing*, Vol. 5, No. 2, pp. 127-45.

ORGANISATION FOR ECONOMIC CO-OPERATION AND DEVELOPMENT

The OECD is a unique forum where governments work together to address the economic, social and environmental challenges of globalisation. The OECD is also at the forefront of efforts to understand and to help governments respond to new developments and concerns, such as corporate governance, the information economy and the challenges of an ageing population. The Organisation provides a setting where governments can compare policy experiences, seek answers to common problems, identify good practice and work to co-ordinate domestic and international policies.

The OECD member countries are: Australia, Austria, Belgium, Canada, Chile, the Czech Republic, Denmark, Estonia, Finland, France, Germany, Greece, Hungary, Iceland, Ireland, Israel, Italy, Japan, Korea, Luxembourg, Mexico, the Netherlands, New Zealand, Norway, Poland, Portugal, the Slovak Republic, Slovenia, Spain, Sweden, Switzerland, Turkey, the United Kingdom and the United States. The European Union takes part in the work of the OECD.

OECD Publishing disseminates widely the results of the Organisation's statistics gathering and research on economic, social and environmental issues, as well as the conventions, guidelines and standards agreed by its members.

OECD PUBLISHING, 2, rue André-Pascal, 75775 PARIS CEDEX 16
(10 2015 20 1 P) ISBN 978-92-64-24704-8 – 2015-02

www.ingramcontent.com/pod-product-compliance
Ingram Content Group UK Ltd.
Pitfield, Milton Keynes, MK11 3LW, UK
UKHW051506290926
15471UKWH00008B/1455

9 789264 247048